The
Alchemy of Gardening

The Alchemy of Gardening

JAN HOYLAND

© Jan Hoyland, 2024

Published by Artemisia Press

A CIP catalogue record for this book is available from the British Library.

ISBN 978-1-7390867-0-1

Illustrations used with kind permission of © Ashford Cottage Design

Book layout by Clare Brayshaw

Prepared and printed by:

York Publishing Services Ltd
64 Hallfield Road
Layerthorpe
York YO31 7ZQ

Tel: 01904 431213

Website: www.yps-publishing.co.uk

Contents

Introduction

Both an art and a science, gardening has always been much more than the planting of botanical species to make an aesthetic statement. I've always known this; I'm a gardener. But it was only recently I became aware of just how much more. Gardening is also a search for peace, for solace; a place to stand and wonder and a way of tethering us back to the earth. While we work the soil, we reclaim our rightful place within the natural world and somewhere, somehow, the mundane becomes magical.

I have always had a strong connection to nature, especially as a child. I was never happier than when I was out in the garden, messing about in the soil and picking flowers, much to my mother's horror. She had dearly wanted a daughter whom she could clothe in frilly dresses, not some muddy half feral child who collected worms and tamed snails. Although I lost sight of this relationship with the natural world for a while through my teens and early twenties, eventually the call returned; I decided to become a professional gardener in my late twenties, and attended the local agricultural college to study horticulture. There I learnt to be a 'proper' gardener and I left after three years with a distinction and a yearning to work in some beautiful gardens. I was fortunate to secure a job with the National Trust, first as an assistant gardener and then as head gardener and I worked in several of their incredible properties, honing my craft, for over ten years. After accepting a management role for a private estate back in my Yorkshire homeland, which appeared to offer great prospects for furthering my career, I rapidly found myself becoming disenchanted with life behind a desk, staring at a screen and the endless timetable of meetings, reports and office politics. It became crystal clear to me that just because I was capable of doing this work, it didn't mean that it was the right choice for me. It took me away from what I loved doing most, which was being outside and working hands-on with people and plants, deeply immersed in the seasons, imagining and planting beautiful spaces, creating communities and watching the wildlife around me. I had to decide: was my life simply about promotion, climbing the career ladder and spending time in an office, or could I simply walk away and return to my true calling?

It was a leap of faith.

I dumped the management job, swerved off the career path and started my own small business as a garden designer, consultant and tree inspector. At the same time, my long-held dream – of actually owning somewhere to develop as a productive smallholding – became a reality. I found a remote and rural patch of land I could just afford, with a semi-derelict cottage, 2 miles down a track, not far from the coast. I began, tentatively, to live my dream, working with my partner to make the cottage habitable and create a garden from scratch. It was exhilarating, but exhausting. I wasn't feeling well, but kept going; deep into renovating the house, while living in a static caravan, I was also helping to care for my mum, who had dementia, as well as trying to keep my new business on track. I was too busy to be ill. But after six months I received a diagnosis that would change my life.

Primary Biliary Cholangitis is a rare auto-immune disorder which I had neither heard of nor could even pronounce. It affects predominantly (but not exclusively) women and causes long term liver disease as the immune system attacks healthy bile duct cells, causing scarring. It was clear that I had been suffering for some years without symptoms, as the damage was considerable. The illness hit me hard. The following winter, we moved into the half-finished cottage; despite the lack of basic amenities, I was too ill to endure another cold season in the caravan.

This sudden plunge into ill health came as a shock. My physical capabilities rapidly diminished; the fatigue made my brain malfunction. I was drained, irritable and grieving my former healthy self. That first winter of illness I plunged into a very dark place, which I kept trying to fight against, but the harder I tried to continue life as I had always lived it, the worse I became. On my darkest days, I bitterly regretted buying up a 'fixer-upper' in 5 acres; my dreams and ambitions for the future were looking decidedly shaky. Despite everything, I continued to plant up my garden in sporadic moments of determined optimism albeit very, very slowly. I planted small trees and shrubs, bought cheaply, into the long and unruly grass. The impetus came more from a stubborn denial of my new reality than out of hope; I was not going to be beaten by this unwelcome turn of events. But with energy levels at rock bottom, unending chronic pain and desperate fatigue I couldn't get through one day without having to stop and rest. While friends and family encouraged me to step back and see the bigger picture, I was close to despair.

Forced to scale back my aspirations, I hid my pain and altered my business model to allow me to continue making a living. While my doctors said there was no cure, that my illness was progressive and would lead to further disability and quite possibly a liver transplant, prescribing tablets which made me feel worse, I told myself I would not give up my dream. I continued, when I could, to plant things in the wilderness.

Gradually, steadily, during this time of enforced not-doing in the garden, moments appeared where I realised that there was in fact a lifeline, a small thread of hope available to me, right under my nose. I started to notice that the only things getting me through the day were the tiny things, the small details of life, offering a minute spark of joy, a glimmer of light when I least expected it. There was solace to be found in this newly diminished environment, my own tiny patch of land. I discovered that far from having a negative impact on the place, this lack of input from me was actually beneficial. My education in horticulture had taught me that gardens required constant work in order to keep on top of them and that any amount of neglect, intentional or otherwise would result in disaster. This was proving to be far from the truth.

As I learnt to listen more carefully to my body in order to understand what I needed to be well again, I also learnt to observe and listen to the land. My gardening interventions were small and slow. My energy levels and health fluctuated by the day and I learnt eventually to work with these cycles, finding a new rhythm to my life. I was forced by my lack of stamina into spending more time watching and less time doing. This switch from an active to a more passive role as gardener lead me towards some startling insights. I learnt that I didn't need to micro-manage the plants I had put in the ground, that nature really just wants to be allowed to get on with the job of growth and change, and that by taking a back seat in the proceedings, the emerging idea of a garden still managed to find a way to turn slowly into the vision I held on to in my mind. Following that first winter of illness, and in the emergence of the first spring blooms, nature taught me how to cultivate hope, from the most barren and unlikely of conditions.

Not everything I planted survived the experience, the growing conditions are far from ideal on this northern moorland edge, yet some did thrive and I experimented widely to come up with ways to garden with the least amount of physical activity. Five years on, my health is gradually beginning to improve and the garden I dreamed of is starting to emerge from the wilderness, slowly but surely, like a developing photograph. The doctors now inform me that I appear to be defying their expectations, as my symptoms are in retreat and my body is beginning to heal a little. While I will always have a malfunctioning immune system that requires careful monitoring and medication, it seems that the damage done is now repairing itself a little, allowing me to function a fraction more easily and without as much pain and fatigue as I originally suffered. The medical staff ask me what my secret is, yet smile kindly when I try to explain. While they joke that they would like to be able to bottle some of my positive attitude to living with chronic illness, they don't seem to understand that being in tune with the seasons, growing and eating home-grown organic produce, and being immersed in a profound appreciation of the wilder side of nature was all the remedy I needed. I am deeply grateful to the wonderful NHS and my medical team for supporting me in my illness, but I also thank nature for providing me with the inspiration and encouragement to stubbornly continue my work on the land despite the limitations I encountered.

Every day, I am reminded that sometimes doing less in the garden, rather than more, is sufficient to create a place of beauty. The wildlife is returning to my once depleted patch of land and I grow fruit and vegetables which provide for my household needs for a good deal of the year. I am so grateful for my privilege in being able to forge a deeper and more harmonious relationship with this plot of land and for being able to share it with the other wild beings which call this place home. I have stretched and tested myself and my imaginings further than I thought possible. I have become more than casually acquainted with nature's ability to heal both the damaged land and my own body, simply by working in co-operation and with mutual respect, rather than against each other as competitors. At a time when I didn't believe that I had anything particularly new to learn about gardening, I found myself amazed by the ability of nature to step into the breach, just at the point when I had nothing left to contribute. I didn't follow many of the traditional rules of horticulture that I had been taught as a student and initially I planted things more with hope than expectation. I had in my head still a vision of how my garden might look, but in the early years of being here and being quite ill, the buying and planting felt like a foolish endeavour, as the grass swamped everything and the weeds flourished. Yet now I understand that nature encourages this approach. We don't need to be quite as controlling as we have been led to believe, in order to get good results when we are planting a garden. I have learnt that if we take our time, learn from what we see happening around us and get to know the plants and non-human beings which share our space while observing the lessons of seasonal change, that we can achieve considerably more than we have been taught to expect.

I have learnt about working in tune with the rhythms of the seasons by following the Celtic calendar, or wheel of the year, with its celebrations and festivals of every aspect of a year on the land. This is an older way of marking the time, of observing the days, months and seasons and it was once widely observed across the British Isles before the Romans arrived on these shores. It is orientated around the summer and winter solstice and spring and autumn equinox days, and it additionally marks the cross-quarter days, which fall between them. I enjoy the celebrations of the seasons, as it teaches me to be grateful for each aspect of our temperate climate and I feel this brings me closer to the rhythms of being and living with a deeper connection to the land we inhabit. It acts as a reminder that we too are seasonal creatures, our energies ebb and flow in harmony with the natural world and this helps me to understand my own inherent nature and assists me in working in a more immersive way with the tools of our trade: the plants, the earth and the creatures I encounter on a daily basis. It helps me to show gratitude for these way-markers throughout the seasons, each one highlighting the wonders of the cycle of birth, growth, harvest, death and rebirth with which we work. This feels, to me, a more holistic approach to gardening and one which is more in line with how our forebears worked the land. The time of turning our backs on nature is over and we can relearn that the magic emerges and unfurls if we allow it to; we simply need to accept that we are not the ones in charge. We are enablers and artists when we create a garden and yet we can make problems for ourselves and others, if we think we are the ones in control, here on the earth.

I am still in the fortunate position of spending much of my time with my hands in the soil and my head in the clouds, while I sow and plant and ponder things. I have learnt a lot about how to garden with a light touch, minimum effort and simply a strong desire to reverse the damage we see around us. I have often wondered if we gardeners have become part of the problem, causing, albeit unwittingly, some of the environmental difficulties that we face today. I have begun to understand, after many years, that some of the things taught to me at college were misguided and that some of what we were told was wrong, or at best only partly truthful. I have explored alternative approaches and tried them for myself and discovered what works for me and my little patch of ground. In my journey towards wellness, I honestly believe I have discovered a better way to garden. I have had plenty of time to consider my role as a gardener and how nature provides for us, with the minimum of effort from ourselves. I propose instead that we can all become part of the solution and begin to fix some of the environmental and social issues which we all face. I am inviting you to join with me to investigate, the often-repeated claim that Nature is the best gardener.

ALCHEMY

CHAPTER ONE

Alchemy

Alchemy

'A seemingly magical process of transformation, creation, or combination.'
'A process that is so effective that it seems like magic.'

Gardening

'The activity of tending and cultivating a garden, especially as a pastime.'
'The job or activity of working in a garden, growing and taking care of the plants, and keeping it attractive.'

The time is ripe for a new role for gardening. In these rapidly changing times, where uncertainty has become an all-too-familiar theme, a garden can be a solace and an anchor in our busy and fractious lives. This alternative approach to gardening can become a source of wonder and a way of rediscovering a deeper appreciation of our own place in the web of life, one which embraces the wilder aspects of nature and the wild kin with which we share the earth. Ever since we began to create gardens to suit our own needs, whether providing rudimentary subsistence living, where people grew the food and medicines they needed, to the grand statements of land ownership made by the wealthy, with their pleasure grounds and parterres, I feel there has been some conflict. Nature was seen as the wild card, uncontrollable, unpredictable and a little bit dangerous. This called for a battle, a war on wild things. Maybe, until recently, gardening has been a useful means for us to experience a sense of the natural world, but it was often on our own terms and always ensuring we are the ones in control. It seems we made a mistake and took a wrong turn somewhere back in the history of gardening and I want to look at the possibilities of gardening in a more regenerative and sustainable way. One which not only heals the damage we humans have inflicted on the environment but one that also provides healing for ourselves and our communities. We can help tackle our disconnection from the natural world and the associated stresses and despair that we can experience in our modern lifestyles. This might sound like wishful thinking, but I'm not sure that should ever prevent us from trying. I am inviting you to discover for yourself a source of magical alchemy in our own gardens by turning some of the horticultural dogmas on their heads and experimenting with a more holistic and hands-off approach.

Unless you have been a hermit for the last few decades, you will be already painfully aware of the environmental catastrophe which we are currently facing. We have lost 97 per cent of wildflower meadows in the UK since the 1930s, and 70 per cent of ancient woodland and 50 per cent of hedgerows since the end of the Second World War. The diversity and variety of wildlife within these habitats has also been damaged or depleted and as a society we are much the poorer for these losses, as we continue to pour concrete over the wildness. In the last fifty years, we have lost one-third of all of the life on the planet. It is often at this point that people begin to feel disempowered by the magnitude of the task ahead of us. How on earth can we stop such wanton degradation and destruction? Can any of us make a difference? We can only make small changes as individuals and surely that won't matter in the great scheme of things. Despair begins to creep in around the edges, so rather than face up to the grief we feel, we resolve to carry on regardless, buy something nice to cheer ourselves up. 'Surely the scientists will come up with something to save us at the last minute,' we think to ourselves and therefore, 'business as usual' becomes our mantra as we continue to follow the wrong path.

In the twenty-first century, almost everywhere we look, nature is in retreat. It doesn't have to be like this, we do still have some agency and a voice we can use to make change occur. The world is in a poor state but things will only continue to get worse unless each of us does our best to change that situation. As gardeners, with temporary stewardship of our tiny plots of earth, is there still a need for conflict with nature, or are we able to imagine a more harmonious relationship where we understand and celebrate our kinship with wild? Perhaps closer co-operation can lead us both to a better place, where both gardener and nature can benefit from a collaboration, with reciprocal benefits for all involved. I want to invite you to explore the practices and methods available to us in achieving this goal and suggest those which I have discovered to be most beneficial in this journey. Permaculture, organics, no-dig gardening and rewilding are all terms you will have heard of, but how do they help us in our quest for the alchemy of gardening, if at all, and how can we utilise them? Perhaps we can we change our ways and become apprentices to the natural world, rather than adversaries. Maybe we can have our lovely gardens without all that hard work or all those chemicals we can buy at the garden centre. Perhaps it's time to be radical and re-imagine the garden and what it means to us. This is the search for the alchemy of gardening, a magical and creative process but one which is firmly based in science and ecology.

Our Lady's Mantle

I first came across the garden's associations with alchemy quite unexpectedly, when I began to learn some old stories and myths behind the naming of species, in preparation for giving a tour of a public garden I was working in. I was researching the plants I intended to talk about and my attention was grabbed by a plant called lady's mantle. It is an all-too-common garden species, but a favourite of mine, rightly famous for its acid froth of green-yellow flowers and an indomitable, some might say invasive, habit. It goes by the more formal Latin name of *Alchemilla mollis*. I discovered that its scientific name was entirely due to its associations with alchemy, as the word *Alchemilla* means 'the little alchemist.' In the past it was thought the dew drops which formed on its leaves were the purest available form of water and were, therefore, considered an essential ingredient for the preparation of potions. It was claimed the magical properties bestowed by this plant via the dew drops were many, ranging from the conjuring of precious substances from ordinary ingredients, to creating spells which were designed to bewitch a man or woman to fall in love with you. I was intrigued!

Alchemilla mollis, I discovered, was also originally sacred to the earth goddess. Its common name of lady's mantle was a later intervention by Christians to associate the plant with the Virgin Mary, eschewing the links to the older earth-based religions and the alchemists of old.

As I dived further down the rabbit hole of investigation, it seems the original study of alchemy was a quest for knowledge on how to transmute or change one element into another, often by trying to turn base metals, such as lead, into gold. Another different branch of alchemists was concerned with discovering the Elixir of Life, which granted a person eternal youth and was a universal cure for all disease, which was, I suspect, ultimately the search for human immortality. It was a strange and archaic blending of science and philosophy and it was primarily practised during medieval times, by a very secretive group of learned and curious people. These shadowy characters and their arcane experiments were the forerunners of the modern science of chemistry. Alchemists spoke in strange secret languages and only discussed their business amongst each other, for fear of being thought of as heretics in a world where religious dogma was the only accepted narrative. They were, of course, pioneering change makers and their experiments eventually allowed others to step outside of the old ways of thinking, allowing new ideas and behaviour to emerge. As we know, human society has changed dramatically since those days, although the change has not been without its problems.

Plants are alchemists

Plants are, of course, the perfect example of alchemy in action. We often take their presence for granted in our lives, but the way they are capable of transforming sunlight, water and carbon dioxide into sugars, energy and growth, is barely short of a miracle. The process of photosynthesis utilises a few very ordinary elements and mysteriously converts them into leaves, stems, roots and flowers. Even the oxygen that we breathe and much of the food that we eat relies upon this. We seldom think about it, once we have moved on from our school biology lessons, but I really want to remind you that this phenomenon underpins the entirety of life on earth. Ecologists call plants 'primary producers', because the complex food chain which supports all organic life on earth, is dependent on the fact that most plants are edible by something and are therefore the original source of energy which supports us all. No wonder then that alchemists were keen to use plants in their experiments. While you might think that these old guys were crazy, and perhaps they were, it is understandable that faced with the knowledge that plants seem to survive solely on sunlight and soil, that some sort of magic is afoot and that maybe by using plants they could harness that energy. This aspect is reinforced when we realise that plants aren't simply a uniform and predictable product which can feed creatures higher up the food chain but that they do this in a mind-boggling number of ways. That plants exist in forms ranging from immense and incredible long-lived trees down to the most miniscule of niche-dwelling alpine specimens, all of them with a bewildering variety of leaf colour, form, flower and fruit, is also quite miraculous. Not only is Mother Nature a benevolent alchemist, but she does it with such phenomenal beauty, creativity and diversity too.

The practice of alchemy has been described as 'taking something ordinary and turning it into something extraordinary, often in a way that cannot be explained'. For me, this sums up not only alchemy but the creation and practice of gardening too. Gardens are frequently capable of being places which become much more than the simple sum of their ingredients. We all recognise that some gardens exude a certain magic, whether this is a subtle feeling of calm and peacefulness, or else a joyfully verdant and dynamic space, rich in beauty and vitality. Many wild places also have the feeling of something mystical and enigmatic about them. We have all walked into a woodland and found ourselves tiptoeing quietly, our senses on full alert, all the while being aware of a wave of tranquility and reverence passing through us as we spend time immersed in the wild landscape. Some gardens are equally capable of echoing these experiences of wild places, allowing us to access this nature connection just outside our door. This, then, feels like alchemy at play and I firmly believe that these created sanctuaries are a wonderful collaboration between ourselves and nature. If gardening is indeed a form of alchemy, then nature is there to teach us how to practise it.

Magic is a concept that we are encouraged to leave behind in childhood, but there is good reason for us to have a little more magic and enchantment in our lives again and it is most definitely not just for children. Nature can be an inspiring source for rediscovering our magical thinking if we are courageous enough to allow it. The alchemists of old grew gardens in order to provide them with the herbs they needed to carry out their spells and experiments, allowing them to harvest the energy and mystery of plants. I wonder if magic and enchantment still play an important role in our gardens, or even if it is even possible for us to think this way in our disciplined and methodical modern world. Perhaps the alchemists were on to something, that maybe plants and nature are still capable of providing us with things we seek, such as wonder, awe and healing. Perhaps we have forgotten some of the things our ancestors knew and understood about the world and maybe we could recreate the search for alchemy of some sort by pushing boundaries and allowing others to change their ways and view the world differently.

Why do we still garden?

In a time-poor society, why on earth would we choose to spend our time doing physical and repetitive work? Gardening may be a great hobby for retired people with time on their hands, or those who like to show off their abilities on social media, but for many, it is enough to be able to hold down a job, pay the bills and put food on the table, without making more work for ourselves. This is a refrain I hear frequently as an excuse for putting down plastic membrane and covering it with gravel as a space for the car. Personally, I think gardening is worth a little more effort on our part with many rewards and dividends; please let me explain.

Somehow, time works differently when we connect with nature, whether in wild places or in the garden. It flows more slowly and allows us to become aware of a more cyclical and seasonal rhythm to life, rather than the more familiar linear time with its demanding deadlines, schedules and associated anxiety. Time in the garden, be it working or simply just being, is like a form of meditation. Nature teaches us to be patient and to find the beauty in small things. Spending time in the garden is often our most convenient and closest link with the natural world and it is this which compels many of us to find the space in our daily schedules to carry out gardening tasks. The pressing sense of time and urgency fades away, as we are absorbed in the simple routines of growing, sowing, weeding and pruning. The hours can slip by, our minds elsewhere while we experiment with creating our perfect symphony with the natural world, using flowers and leaves as the melodies and harmonies. This can be the perfect therapeutic antidote to our frantic and stressful work-filled lives. Time spent gardening is never wasted.

We should begin by rethinking what a garden means to us. It could be much more than the bald patch of gravel for parking the car, or a rectangle of scruffy grass where the kids can kick a ball or the dog can go for a wee. We can choose to bring a more bewitching image of our relationship with the wild world outside our door a little closer. If we can learn to work alongside nature, it doesn't even have to create much extra work and indeed over time, a well-thought-out garden can be almost self-maintaining. It can be our way of doing something positive in a world of negative and often overwhelming news.

Where did we go wrong?

The utopian vision of a vegetable plot with everything in neat rows, or an immaculate and meticulous flower border, with colour all through the season and no sign of a weed anywhere, appears to be the current zenith of attainment. I do admire the people who are willing to put in the extreme effort to achieve this standard of control at home, although to me it appears out of balance. Sadly, it seems, however, that we can't get enough of it and a whole industry has sprung up in order to further convince us that the perfect garden is not only desirable but achievable too. Scratch at the surface of this illusion and you will soon realise that not only does it take an awful lot of effort but often an entire arsenal of weed killer, pesticides, fungicides and fertilisers. Just visit any garden centre and you will be bombarded by shelves of chemical fixes to solve any gardening problem you might have.

Garden centres and online plant sellers are where most people buy their garden plants, but they can be a fatal distraction, as the bright and shiny flowers enticing us to buy them are not always our best choices. We have all been seduced by the colourful pages of mail order catalogues, sent to us at the start of the growing year, when we are starved of colour and floral excitement. Many of these plants have been grown pumped up on artificial fertilisers, extra heat and light and pesticides, all in order to bring them to you in peak condition. Once they are placed out into our gardens, such plants go into shock as they struggle to adapt to the real-world conditions they find themselves in. Many don't make it and leave you needing to buy more, a clever trick from the consumerist handbook, where more money is spent on marketing than on good plant husbandry. Those plants that do survive can actually cause problems to the native insects which share your garden space, because their pesticide burden can act as a slow poison to a wide range of insects, many of which we now revere, such as bees and butterflies.

People who have grown up with this approach to gardening may even come to consider nature and wildlife as the cause of their problems when it comes to seeking perfection. This is the mindset which sees weeds instead of wild flowers, all insects as pests, and fungi as the cause of diseases. Such gardeners struggle to grasp the concept that these insects and fungi are an intrinsic part of the complex web of life which underpins the whole of the garden ecosystem and beyond. This thinking leads to plastic weed barriers put down under decorative mulches to ensure that only the right plants have the opportunity to grow, with nothing in between, in the misguided belief that there is such a thing as a low-maintenance garden. This approach flies in the face of what should happen in a natural, balanced system and leads to a poorly functioning plot, which results in sick plants and exasperated gardeners. It is a sad legacy we have inherited and it doesn't have to be this way.

CHAPTER TWO

Samhain

The end of October might feel like a strange time to begin a book about gardening, just as everything is starting to slow down at the end of the growing season as we transition from autumn to winter. In the Celtic wheel of the year, our ancestors celebrated Samhain as the end of the old year and the beginning of the new one. It was during this time that the veil between the worlds of the living and the dead was at its thinnest, allowing us to make closer connections to our ancestors and those who went before us. This is mirrored in the garden, as the bountiful days of summer have ended and the slow retreat into winter has begun. The death and decay of the plants and foliage in our gardens acts as a reminder to us that in the great circle of living, everything must come to an end. It marks a quieter time in the gardener's life; it allows us to slow down and contemplate the year – a time of remembering and thinking of those who trod this patch of earth before us. A time to look inwards and learn from the well of wisdom and knowledge which has been passed on to us. It is a good time to make plans and sow the seeds of new ideas and projects as the dark winter days allow us the time to dream. I would like to invite you to shed your old leaves of gardening ideas, to cast aside any unwanted prejudices about gardening with nature, to compost what you used to do in the garden and prepare yourself and your patch of earth for a new beginning by embracing dormancy and quietly germinating seeds of hope.

Samhain is a poignant time for me as this was when, in 2021, I was given the news that my chronic illness was in retreat. I vividly remember the incredible wave of relief and disbelief that flowed through me as I drove home from the hospital and the full meaning of the consultant's words slowly began to sink in. I remember that I stopped off for a walk in the woods on the way home, to give me time and space to process fully what I had been told. The woods were still in their peak of autumn glory as there had been no frosts to hasten the leaves to fall and the scent of sweet damp earth pervaded. Despite it being a dull and overcast day with the light beginning to fade, the golds, rusts and russets of the dying foliage seemed almost to glow with an internal light. Walking in woodland is always my preferred solution to anything that makes me feel emotional. Being in the presence of trees offers me sanctuary, grounds me by making me more present in the moment and soothes my chattering brain. I remember that I sat for some time, I'm not sure how long, on a damp, moss-clad log at the side of the track and allowed the feelings to pass through me. I cried as I began to realise I had been given a second chance. My fear that my life was destined to be one of progressive ill health and a long wait on a transplant list began to diminish and my heart felt so full I thought it would burst. For a while longer, I just sat and felt supported in nature until I was ready to face the world again.

I'm not the first person to have benefited from the therapeutic presence of trees. Increasingly, we are learning that spending time in and around trees and woodland is good for our mental health. The Japanese call this Forest Bathing or more poetically *Shinrin-yoku*, a form of eco therapy which not only is free and incredibly simple to use but which also encourages us to have a vested interest in the presence and health of our natural environment. Scientists have discovered that trees, and some soil organisms, exude minute amounts of organic chemical compounds from their leaves, which we breathe in as we walk, this being the distinctive yet indescribable scent of woodlands we are all familiar with. These compounds are processed through inhalation and affect our brains and bodies. They enable our mood to improve, decrease mental fatigue and increase cognitive ability, while offering antioxidant and anti-inflammatory benefits, as we relax in nature. Perhaps if we planted more trees in our towns and cities we might be able to feel a little less stressed as we go about our work.

The days between Samhain at the end of October and Imbolc at the start of February, are perfect for planning what it is you want to do in the garden ... an auspicious time to plan a little alchemy. When I first moved to my current garden, it was early January and I spent my time walking the waterlogged land wearing wellies and wrapped in in multiple layers of clothing. Standing, staring and imagining how it could look were the main pursuits that marked my early days of being a smallholder and landowner.

Genius

Once you learn to simply spend time in your garden without feeling the need to do anything in particular, it may be that you will find an unexpected source of inspiration to help you in your endeavours. I personally find having a walk around the garden is a fabulous way to make decisions about all sorts of things, not just those with a horticultural theme. Try asking the garden what it most needs and it might be surprise you when the answer comes back sooner than you think. Contacting the genius of the place sounds like a crazy idea but maybe it isn't. In ancient Rome, the word genius was understood to mean a guiding spirit or deity which was associated with a person or place. Therefore, someone who was extra talented or creative in some way was said to 'have a genius'. The later use of the word, describing someone with exceptional talent as 'being a genius', has overtaken the original intention behind the term. One of the first written references to this was by the poet and gardener Alexander Pope in the 1700s in his book *Epistles to Several Persons* where he spoke clearly about the need to consult the genius of the place or *Genius Loci* as a primary source of ideas for designing a landscape garden. I am inclined to agree with him.

Naturally, I'm not suggesting you necessarily need to summon a deity in order to work in your garden or design the layout of your vegetable plots. Such beliefs might result in your neighbours deciding to call the police due to your strange behaviour or your loved ones thinking that you needed a holiday or to speak to a doctor! However, I do wonder if there is something in this idea of places having spirit. I am sure we have all walked into a woodland or ambled along a beach and found ourselves transported in our heads to a place so much more joyous and life enhancing than you would expect it to be. There are plenty of folk tales and legends which talk about nature spirits: Jack in the Green; the Green Man; and even Robin Hood. Perhaps all this is a convenient way to let us know that sometimes we are just acting as channels for creativity and magic, whether this is art, music or gardening and that there is a genius lurking behind a tree, who comes up with all the best ideas – if we would only just shut up and listen for a bit.

One day while I was carrying out a tree survey in a school playground, I found myself surrounded by curious children. A small girl came up to me and demanded to know why I was hitting the tree with a hammer. 'I'm trying to wake it up, so I can tell it spring is coming', I said. She nodded sagely and then whispered to me conspiratorially, 'There are fairies living in that tree.' 'I know', I answered. 'I can hear them singing'. Smiling broadly, she skipped away happy that the tree was in no danger. A few minutes later, I was accosted by an old lady who lived in an adjacent bungalow. Shouting across to me she complained, 'Those trees are a damn disgrace; I hope they are coming down.' I answered that they were doing well, were in excellent health and that I had no intention of condemning them. 'What about the leaves, such a terrible mess they make, you have no idea what a nuisance those trees are.' I smiled and tried to explain the importance of trees to the natural environment and how they even help to make the air we breathe. The old lady narrowed her eyes, took a puff of her cigarette and shuffled back indoors, muttering under her breath. It left me wondering about trees, nature's role in our lives, and when and why we stop believing in magical things. I am pretty sure that it isn't entirely age related but, somehow, I think we need to find our way back to enchantment, no matter how old we are. Nature is relying on us.

Permaculture

Throughout my years of being a professional gardener, as well as during my time of planting and planning a garden here, I have tried various methods and theories of natural gardening. I have read extensively about rewilding practices and organic and regenerative principles and incorporated them into what I do. We have an overload of information available to us these days via the internet, and sometimes it can be difficult to know what might be practical and useful to our situation and which could be useful perspectives we can adapt to suit our needs.

The ethos behind my personal approach to gardening now has its roots deeply embedded in permaculture thinking. I first learnt about permaculture as a nature-obsessed young person, when I used to volunteer to carry out conservation tasks in my home town and it was here that I first heard the term used. It impressed me enough to want to learn more, as it appeared to offer a lot of practical solutions to environmental issues. It was a topic which kept cropping up in many aspects of my life, both professionally and personally, and I began to buy books to read to learn more about how this all worked. Much later, while living and working in Cornwall, I went on to take my permaculture design certificate. It is one of the most useful concepts I have been taught and although it is becoming more mainstream these days, is a practice still predominantly used for just growing food. I have used permaculture myself, more as a lens through which to view gardening, not only as a means of designing a place from scratch but also as a framework for creating and maintaining both the ornamental and productive aspects of my own garden and those I design for others. I can honestly say that it changed my life for the better.

Permaculture is an ecologically based design process. It was originally devised in the 1970s by two Australian men, Bill Mollinson and David Holmgren, and it has blossomed and expanded across the world since then. The name comes from a contraction of the two words 'permanent agriculture', as it was initially intended to be used in the design of permanent and sustainable agricultural systems. While it is still predominantly used as a design tool in garden and farm settings, it can also be used to inform the design of buildings, businesses, lifestyles and products and it is now widely used across many countries for a wide variety of purposes. Heather Jo Flores, permaculture teacher and writer, sums it up beautifully for me saying: 'Permaculture is about personal responsibility, thoughtful action and careful ecological design. It is about science, evidence and results.'

Based on imitating naturally occurring and sustainable systems in nature, such as forests with their many layers of vegetation, it has close similarities to the farming practices of many indigenous peoples across the globe, who often worked much more closely with natural processes than our modern society does. These long-established and harmonious ways of farming and living off the land existed for countless generations in a variety of communities around the world, long before industrial agriculture came to be the accepted way of growing food.

Permaculture design uses a series of ethics and principles to guide and inform the design process. The ethics are simply those of Earth Care, People Care and Fair Shares and they underpin all decision making and design and really speak for themselves. Caring for the earth is something that should be intrinsic in all our considerations and we should aim to be the best stewards of this unique place that we call home, that we can be.

The underpinning philosophy of 'People Care' is that we should treat everyone as equal to ourselves and all decision making should ensure that everyone is treated fairly and equitably. After all, we all share the same wants, needs and aspirations. Although we could start with self-care as a basic idea, we can naturally expand this to include family, friends and community. That this community should stretch to encircle all people who live on the planet, as well as our non-human kin, should go without saying.

'Fair Shares' is the ethic that asks that we only take what we need to fulfil our needs, leaving sufficient for others, whether human or wildlife, and that we ensure that we think about future generations and their needs as well as our own. Setting limits should be seen to be normal behaviour, with the redistribution of any surplus to others being a natural outcome. A secure future for all should be at the heart of everything we do, as robbing Peter to pay Paul is never an effective strategy for the long term, despite the current social discourse of self-interest and wealth accumulation, which might suggest otherwise.

The twelve principles are a series of tools or steps to consider when you are engaged in designing, creating or decision making:

1.   Observe and interact
2.   Catch and store energy
3.   Obtain a yield
4.   Apply self-regulation and accept feedback
5.   Produce no waste
6.   Use and value renewables and resources
7.   Design from pattern to detail
8.   Integrate rather than segregate
9.   Use small and slow solutions
10. Use and value diversity
11. Use edges and value the marginal
12. Creatively use and respond to change

At first, not all these principles will seem to be pertinent to everything you are trying to achieve, but as you spend some time considering them, it can often help you come up with simple and elegant solutions to thorny problems. I will work with these principles and introduce them to you within a practical context as we travel through a year in the garden.

Being taught these permaculture principles and ethics as a framework for planning, designing and working in the garden has been, for me, a helpful toolkit. I still make mistakes by rushing into things but the art of experimentation doesn't always mean that you will get things right first time. Luckily for us gardeners, nature is extremely forgiving and usually has the ability to put things back on track if we admit our failures and allow her to rediscover the correct path, so that we can learn from our errors. Permaculture often tends to concentrate on the edible and productive aspects of gardening, rather than ornamental or leisure spaces, but this doesn't mean that we can't use the same principles to inform our decision-making process while creating something of beauty.

November brings gales, fog and the first frosts. I pull on my trusty wellies, big padded jacket and go outside, despite my initial reluctance. On days like these, it's hard to find the positives and the dismal skies and cold winds don't always make for the best reasons to be outdoors. I dislike the winter with its fleeting days and long nights, yet I find that even a half hour of being in nature can have a profoundly positive impact on my mood. I sort through the remains of the bulb order I put together back in the summer and decide where I will plant them. I enjoy planting bulbs; it takes little effort and the rewards arrive relatively quickly, the closest to instant gardening I ever manage. Every year I think I have enough spring bulbs, yet when it comes to ordering them for my design customers, I always find myself adding a few extra for myself … all in the name of research, you understand. After an hour of planting, I feel weary so I return to the fireside, eject the cat from the chair, make myself a coffee and congratulate myself for having made the effort.

Permaculture principle: Observe and interact

This is the first permaculture principle we will examine and perhaps, in my opinion at least, the most important. The principle encourages us to take notice of natural systems and communities and interact with them to learn more about how we can create sustainable outcomes. Observation is of course incredibly useful at the start of collaborating with nature, but it should also be carried out throughout our tenure, as the gardens we are creating together will change over time and therefore our responses should be able to adapt appropriately. Making small and considered interactions should be our intention, followed by careful observation so that we can learn from the changes taking place. It is important to realise that making mistakes while gardening can be a very useful tool, as long as we are able to recognise that we have gone about things wrongly and that we are able to learn from our mistakes.

Getting acquainted with the land on which you garden can take many forms. Learning where the sunniest spots are and where the frosts sit longer than anywhere else, are all lessons in microclimate. This is understanding the specific parts of the garden where conditions are different from the rest. This is usually about the amount of sunlight an area receives although it can also be affected by the wind, which affects the temperature of an area. Understanding the type of soil you will be gardening with is just as essential and digging a few holes to more closely examine soil types can also be a useful exercise. Soils tend to fall into categories depending on what their main constituents are, usually either clay or sand. This will allow you to choose plants which suit the circumstances in which they will be living. The principle of 'observe and interact' is very much at play here, which teaches us that getting to know the land we are living on is perhaps the first and most important stage of gardening.

In order to observe, it is useful to slow ourselves down. As a professional gardener, this was one of the things I found the hardest to do, especially when someone is paying you to be productive. I can only imagine what some of my line managers would have said to me if they had found me sitting and pondering in a sunny corner of the garden, rather than dealing with my never-ending to-do list. While I was always aware of the need to match my pace to that of nature's own, – in order to fully be aware of the changes taking place – it was only when I became too ill to carry out much physical work that I fully understood how important it was to take the time to observe. I have learnt that lesson now, and even though I am paid to design and create gardens for other people, I ensure that sufficient time is spent watching, feeling and exploring the space before I even measure it up. I encourage my clients to do the same, to truly get a feel for the land, however small and mundane it might seem at first. It is only when we experience a place in all of its seasons and moods that we can work with nature to create a place which is sustainable and ecologically sound.

Observing and interacting also brings us health benefits. We all spend rather too much of our time indoors, often under artificial light or staring at screens which can over stimulate our brains and even disrupt our sleep patterns; in contrast, natural light can help us feel calmer, more able to focus. Being out in the garden also presents the chance for joyful encounters with nature which can make you smile. Seeing a bird up close, such as a cheeky robin hopping around in the undergrowth, watching to see if you have disturbed any insects, can be a wonderfully intimate connection with nature. A scientific study in 2020 discovered that the more types and numbers of birds a person has contact with, the happier they report feeling. If you want to feel even happier in your gardening life, perhaps you could work out whereabouts you can put up an extra bird feeder or nest box in order to boost your chances of finding happiness.

Caught in the rat race

Modern life is absurd. We live in ways which are so disconnected from nature that we forget that we are part of the web of life. Still, we tell ourselves that since we must work to pay the bills, we deserve to spend a little money on ourselves, we deserve a new outfit or a trip to the cinema to see the latest release. We dash from one task to another because being busy is now a badge of honour. We use our busyness as an excuse for not taking the time to see friends or go for a walk, or even just sit for five minutes and listen to the birds singing in the park or garden. We get stuck in the fast lane of twenty-first century life. A constant striving for progress, more stuff, more experiences. As our lives speed up to embrace the norms of a twenty-first century lifestyle, it becomes ever more difficult to appreciate the small things. In the hustle of making ends meet, we have lost ourselves and failed to realise that the world we live in is ruled by natural processes.

It is possible to have a very light footprint in a garden or outdoor space and still have the opportunity to express yourself and be creative. Gardening with nature is an invitation to explore some of the older ways of working with plants and the land. This does not mean we must eschew technology or science, rather that we use the two together to create a deeper understanding. We can think of it as a returning to the old ways, coming back around, full circle, like the seasons. Not going backwards in time, but forwards in a never-ending cycle of renewal. To me, natural gardening feels much more intuitive and can be a way of restoring land to a more fertile and productive state. This in turn encourages wildlife to participate in creating diverse ecosystems and habitats within our own gardens.

In inviting nature to play a part in your garden, you might discover that this can cultivate a sense of chaos to your once ordered and controlled surroundings. Initially, you might find this a bit disconcerting, but once you allow yourself to stand back and reduce your managerial role within the garden, beautiful things can begin to happen. There is an old saying which goes 'Despite the gardeners' best intentions, Nature will always improvise.' A splash of unexpected colour from a self-seeded wilding, or a beautiful contrast of foliage in the autumn can be as life affirming as any uplifting piece of music. Doing the bare minimum could well be the key that turns a garden from the mundane to the magical.

December has arrived, with frosts and snow, along with the fieldfares, a handsome, thrush-like bird which over winters in the UK. I pick through the apples I have stored in the shed and pick out a few which are beginning to wizen and rot. I put them on the ground near the bird feeders and before long the garden is full of bickering blackbirds and our feathered migrant friends, feasting on the sweet juicy fruit. The ground is frozen hard and the cold wind ruffles my hair, making me shiver as I top up the feeders, which hang in the old plum tree, with sunflower hearts and fat balls for the smaller birds who dislike the tussle and strife of life amongst the ground feeders. The hedgerows round and about have already been flailed by over-eager farming contactors in the pursuit of tidiness which has now come to plague the countryside, robbing the birds of their winter larder.

I decide I will plant a rowan tree in the hope of attracting some waxwings, another Scandinavian visitor to our shores, which boast a jazzy crest of feathers atop their head and beautiful plumage. The birdwatching groups on social media are full of pictures of a flock of them in our local town, congregating in a shopping centre carpark, where there is surprisingly plenty of food and cover for them. The berries of the rowan are one of their preferred foods and the tree is perfect for a small garden, with its frothy white flowers in May and exquisite autumn colour. A very hardy tree, it seems to grow in most types of soil, doesn't mind shade and best of all doesn't become too large. There are lots of varieties to choose from with berries which range in colour from scarlet through pink, yellow and white. The red-berried ones, however, are always the birds' favourites. I go back indoors to light the woodburning stove and do some research on the internet about the different types of rowans available and become distracted by the range of other bird-friendly small trees as I consider where I could fit a few more trees into the space I have. I then discover that there are some wonderful varieties of crab apple and hawthorn too, which provide beautiful and nutritious berries and these are dutifully added to my tree-planting wish list.

Watch and listen carefully

Let us begin again with the gentle art of observation. Learn to appreciate your garden in all its aspects, seasons and moods. One of the most important skills to have as a gardener is to be still and watch things closely. This is an important part of gardening and something that we most definitely should not be ashamed of indulging in, even if it looks as though we are being idle. We are very good at getting 'stuck in' to a task, rushing almost, to make a difference, rather than taking our time and allowing the decision-making process to unfold at a pace more appropriate to the natural rhythm of life. This teaches us to contemplate our space and preferably experience it through a full year before making any hard-and-fast decisions. By all means, grow a few things, but mistakes are easily made in the first impulse to get things underway, so don't be daunted if things don't quite live up to your initial expectations. Trial and error can be expensive if you are buying specimens from a garden centre, but experimenting with a few packets of seed is unlikely to break the bank. Growing plants from seed is a slow process too and while it might not give you the initial thrill of buying something ready grown from the garden centre, I can assure you that the delayed gratification of harvesting food or flowers from something you have nurtured from a tiny packet of seed is far more fulfilling.

Taking the time to get to know your garden should be a soothing and meditative process. Take a small stool and move yourself around to sit in different places. Feel free to have a cup of tea while you master this delicate art of being idle. The Vietnamese Buddhist monk Thich Nhat Hanh was a famous proponent of tea drinking and mindfulness. There is a lovely quote by him which states: 'Drink your tea slowly and reverently, as if it is the axis on which the earth revolves – slowly, evenly, without rushing toward the future. Live the actual moment. Only this moment is life.'

Wrap up warm and try doing this on a sunny winter's day. Where is the best place in your garden to sit when the temperatures are low? There is a word for the warmth of the sun in the winter, it is called 'Apricity' and it feels like a lovely warm hug on a cold day. See if you can find somewhere where you can enjoy this feeling, even briefly. I learnt the best places to sit in my own garden by observing where the cat liked to curl up for a nap. Cats are very good at discovering the best microclimates, out of the wind and somewhere warm. Try channelling your inner cat, if you don't have access to a real one, and see if you can discover the gentle art of how to apricate or bask in the warmth of the winter sun. These warm niches are often a great place to plant very early flowers, especially those which have sweet scents, such as winter box (*Sarcococca* species), winter honeysuckle (*Lonicera fragrantissima*) or varieties of *Daphne*.

Try making a plan or map of your garden and doodling some ideas for what you want to achieve. This is a great way to come up with new ideas and try them out on paper first. Mark on that plan where you like to sit, where the birds prefer to gather, where the frost stays all day in winter and where the sun stays longest on midsummer evenings. All of this information will help you decide what types of plants you can grow successfully in the garden and how best to lay out the planting areas.

Basking in the winter sun and warming my bones feels as though I am plugging into the energy of the universe and I take the chance whenever I can to partake in some apricating behaviour.

> *It's midwinter, just over two weeks from the winter solstice. There's a thin layer of snow over everything, like icing sugar on a cake, offsetting the darkness of the day. As I sit at my desk, a wren appears, perching on the edge of a terracotta pot on a table, outside my window. It has been the year for wrens, our stacked firewood pile has been the ideal habitat for a pair of enthusiastic wrens to set up home. They raised an impressive two broods, which meant that I was followed around the garden throughout summer being chided loudly by a busy wren trying to feed her offspring. Today's wren shows no fear of me, as it pecks at the remains of a marguerite daisy, battered by last night's freezing temperatures. Aphids had clothed the stems of the plant for most of the summer, along with the climbing rose trained around the window. I hadn't sprayed them, even with soapy water, and it flowered beautifully despite its botanical hitchhikers. Now those aphids were providing a quick snack for my wren friend and I'm glad I left them. I could so easily have killed the aphid in the pursuit of perfection and I would have denied myself the joy of having had such an intimate encounter with a wren.*

Invitations to celebrate the season

- On the eve of Samhain, consider having a bonfire in your garden if you are allowed to. It doesn't have to be very big and indeed I would encourage you to keep it small. Collect a little bundle of twigs, bound together with string, which represent your hopes for the year ahead. If you can't burn your twig bundle, then leave it in a sheltered nook where it can rot down slowly. Use the ash from the bonfire to add to your compost heap to provide potash for the new growth which will come in the spring.

26

- Collect some autumn leaves and try your hand at creating some art with them on the ground. You can use twigs, berries and seed heads too to make a picture or a design on the ground. I like to make circular mandalas, but feel free to create whatever you choose. Take a photo of it and then let it disappear back into nature, as it blows away or is eaten by worms!

- Sow seeds of those flowers which require a spell of coldness to break their dormancy and allow germination to occur. Plants such as cowslips need to be chilled before they will appear. Many such plants note on their seed packets that you should keep them in the fridge, in a plastic bag of compost for a few weeks, but why not sow them outside and let them experience winter, as nature intended, in a sheltered corner of the garden. I always get much better germination rates by autumn sowing, rather than putting them in the fridge. This process is known as vernalisation.

- This is the time of year to plant garlic. It's one of the easiest vegetables to grow and can be planted in large pots too if you don't have room in the garden. I use garlic bulbs from the supermarket, rather than feeling I need to buy seed garlic from a nursery. Break the bulb into separate cloves and choose the biggest and plumpest cloves to plant. They are very hardy, so don't need any winter protection. You should be harvesting your garlic by around June or July next year. Delicious!

- Collect a few acorns while out walking in the woods and plant them in pots of garden soil. They should germinate next spring. Grow them on for a few months and donate them to a conservation charity or else find somewhere suitable to plant them, where they will have the space to grow into trees. Remember that they make big trees, so be careful not to plant them near to buildings or power lines, where they might become a problem in the future.

CHAPTER THREE

Yuletide

Yule or the winter solstice on 21ˢᵗ December is when the sun is at its weakest here in the north, as it coincides with the shortest day. The garden lays dormant and the land is sleeping, cold and unresponsive. These half-lit days are dim and cloud muffled without a sound of wind nor movement, just a slow sullen silence. The solstice is a time to pause, a time of sacred stillness, as for a few days the nights neither grow longer nor shorter and we are held in suspension before the light begins to return. This is a time to huddle close, to kindle the fires, gather with friends and family, for these are the darkest of days and we must tell each other the stories of the summer to keep them alive.

I invite friends to come for dinner on the longest night of the year. I conjure up a menu which uses as much of my own home-grown vegetables as I can, whether fresh or stored, as a celebration of the abundance and generosity of the earth in providing our food. I also invite them to think about the things they would like to attract or achieve in the year ahead. I ask them to collect twigs from their own garden while they do this, each twig representing a wish for the future. While I also make twig bundles at Samhain, this tends to be a private and deeply personal ritual of the aspects I wish to embody and something I always do alone. At Yule, it's a good reminder for me to revisit my bundle of intention and it's a much more light-hearted and sociable celebration of the return of the sun and a way of looking forward to the year ahead. We each make small bundles of our twiggy dreams and as the sun sets, we light a bonfire and throw on our hopeful bundles and raise our glasses of mulled wine to the return of the sun. We eat, drink and make merry, for this is the time for celebration, gratitude and appreciation for the year we have had and the one yet to come.

The next morning, I contemplate the garden as I walk slowly around it. Stark and intricate in its nakedness, the bare bones are exposed for all to see. There is still so much understated beauty in this pared-back landscape and I appreciate its vulnerability. I find the short dismal days difficult to bear and the long dark nights interminable, with little brightness available to pierce the gloom. My motivation to do anything seeps from me like rain from a heavy cloud and I feel as though I want to sleep until spring. I urge my body to work, do simple tasks, draw breath, stand still and give thanks. I find myself scraping holes and pushing bulbs into the ground. I had forgotten to plant them at the prescribed time and now, months late, I tell myself they stand more chance in the ground than languishing in a mouldy paper bag in the shed. No skill required here, just a vision of better times and I hold on tightly to hope, for all it's worth, finding solace in small things. Silken webs festoon the field in intricate complexities, the remains of seed heads and grassy spikes hang low, bowed by the weight of a thousand tiny droplets, glistening in the pallid light of the setting sun. Turning to watch as the sun slips back below the horizon, my eyes grasp at the shards of dying light as I wait for the return of the sun's reign over the earth.

Nature as inspiration

Mimicking natural systems and habitats can make your garden easier to manage, allowing more time for enjoyment, relaxation and appreciation. For example, bare earth is rarely found in unmanaged places and when it is, nature does her best to cover her modesty as soon as possible. So rather than engaging in a constant warfare against weeds, why not consider filling those areas with plants you really want. Perhaps some of those more peaceful natives we call weeds could be part of the mix? Then the seasonal changes of vegetation can be allowed to ebb and flow as nature intends, allowing for one session of cutting back old decayed growth and plant selection – a phrase I much prefer to 'weeding' – at the start of the growing year. Spring-flowering bulbs will cover the soil in the early months and as these jewels of spring begin to sink back into the ground, the later emerging vegetation will expand to fill those gaps. Allowing a few wildings to set seed and spread around can make for interesting and dynamic borders, which change over time and always have surprises. I particularly like the way violets, poppies, feverfew, forget-me-not and love-in-a-mist all have the virtue of volunteering themselves to fill bare spaces and offer colourful interludes in unexpected ways.

Gardening in a way which is based on observing nature is a case of not only imitating some of what we see but also allowing natural processes to take some of the decisions for us. I am not advocating allowing nettles to rampage through the borders, but I am suggesting that daisies and dandelions in your grassy areas can be left alone to flourish and that maybe you could allow nettles to grow somewhere, even if only at the back of the shed, where you can't see them. Natural gardening is about trying to establish ecosystems in our gardens that closely imitate those we find in the wild. Whether these are woodland ecosystems for shady gardens with a range of shade-tolerant plants, or a meadow-style ecosystem for sunnier sites, we should choose our plants carefully, depending on the aspect, soil type or the microclimates we encounter. We are simply trying to establish suitable and sustainable ecosystems in our gardens which will create beautiful spaces with the minimum of input from the gardener.

Permaculture principle: Use small and slow solutions

This permaculture principle enables us to approach change by taking small steps towards what we are trying to achieve. Since big changes can be difficult to consider in life and have the potential to put people off trying to do anything, due to the magnitude of the problem, this principle encourages us to think small, suggesting that a lot of little steps in the right direction can make a big difference over time. When time or energy are in short supply, making these tiny but considered steps towards a goal allows us to make progress without feeling overwhelmed. Equally, it is also the case that smaller interventions are not only better for the ecosystems we are working with, but that this approach is more beneficial to our mental health too. Smaller systems are more suited to sustainable living: for example, buying locally produced vegetables or cut flowers, or even growing our own, allows for a healthier lifestyle with less energy input and less reliance on large corporations who don't always have our best interests at heart.

Taking small actions should therefore always be our intention, naturally followed by careful observation so that we can learn from the changes taking place. It is important to realise that making mistakes while gardening can be a very useful tool, as long as we are able to recognise that we have gone about things wrongly and we are able to learn from our mistakes. While I was studying to become a gardener, I frequently became exasperated with the contrast between my own love of wild places and the constant battle against nature that gardening seemed to be obsessed with. I originally decided that organic gardening was where my interests lay and that I would pursue this angle to the best of my abilities. When I graduated from college, it became clear that most public gardens at that time used herbicides, pesticides and artificial fertiliser. I had no option other than to use these during my daily work until I managed to get a job as a head gardener for a property. I spoke to the boss about managing the garden organically but was told that it wouldn't be possible to reach the high standards required without the use of chemicals. I continued until we ran out of stocks and then I continued to manage the garden without them, but kept it to myself. After a year, I confessed to my gardening advisor and manager that I was actually gardening organically. They were initially horrified but as they hadn't noticed any difference, they agreed to let me continue for a while longer. I believe this was the first garden within the National Trust to convert to organic principles. Since then, many things have changed and most gardens try to be at least sparing in their use of biocides, which of course is a huge step forward. The garden is still, to this day managed entirely organically.

This principle of small and slow intervention still pretty much sums up my current approach to gardening, especially now that I am limited by the symptoms of my illness and the side effects of the medication I must take. Nature has taught me repeatedly that that sometimes the changes I need to make can be so miniscule as to be almost invisible, yet the effect I can make, over a period of time can be profound. In the early days of living here, when I was really quite poorly, the planting of tiny trees and shrubs, which felt so important to my mental health, also appeared to be a battle against the land which seemed to be on a rewilding journey of its own. Yet now, several years on, most of those plants have survived, grown larger and are beginning to make their own habitat. The ground flora around them is changing, the long grass which was swamping everything with luxuriant growth to begin with is retreating, and my mulching every spring with woodchip is making a much more inviting ecosystem for a wider range of more interesting plants to be introduced.

There is little essential maintenance to do in the garden at this time of the year, thankfully. As the cold temperatures turn the borders into dull, shabby imitations of their summertime glory, this can be a useful time to move plants about, plant new woody shrubs or trees and look at the simpler structures provided by woody plants which form the basis of most gardens.

The first thing I realised in my own garden was that I needed to plant some hedges to give some shelter from the cruel winds which blow across the moors. Luckily, hedging is an easy decision to make; they mark predetermined boundaries and therefore little thinking is required regarding their position. Winter is also a perfect time to plant trees, shrubs or anything woody. I always prefer to buy things bare-rooted, which means they have been grown in a field and lifted just prior to sale without any soil around their roots. This is, I think, the most sustainable way to buy plants – they use no plastic pots, potting compost, peat or fertiliser. I also think they tend to establish more successfully as they don't have to make that transition from growing in artificially nice conditions to having to make their own way in the world. Most native shrubs and trees can be bought this way and they have the added bonus of often being much cheaper than their pot-grown cousins.

Soil

When I first began the planting up of my garden, I quickly realised that our soils were damaged and depleted. This suspicion was proved over time, as the plants I put in the ground sulked and struggled to establish and grow. It was only as I witnessed the farmers who had previously managed this land, repeatedly drive around in their tractors to spray herbicides and scatter artificial fertiliser, that I realised the situation was quite serious and that this would take a while to fix. Our soils are already waterlogged and very acidic, as this land was previously moorland, which had been ploughed up during the 1950s to increase UK food production capabilities. I added manures to the vegetable plot and piles of woodchip around the trees in the hope of boosting the fertility. I eventually realised that the soil lacked the necessary biology to achieve this outcome. There was a worrying lack of life in the soil.

Soil is a living entity, so much more than just dirt. It contains a complex community of organisms, as diverse and dazzling as the rainforests. That thin layer of carbon-rich habitat is as vital to life on earth as oxygen and water. Without a healthy layer of soil between the bedrock and the atmosphere, we simply would not exist. As gardeners, we are more than superficially acquainted with soil, we spend a lot of time with our hands in it and an equal amount of time cursing it and probably wishing we had something more akin to the multipurpose compost that we buy in bags to raise our young plants. It is, however, more complex and interesting than the coloured plastic bags full of sterile manufactured contents, which promise you the super power of being able to grow bigger, better specimens. Soil is a world away from simply being an inert substance made from underlying rocks and a bit of organic matter, providing plants with something to grow in. As a student gardener, I was taught about the chemistry of soil, the nutrients it contains – which feed the plants – and the structures which make up the different types of soil. We learnt the chemical practicalities that many of us have heard about, such as the major nutrients of nitrogen, potassium and phosphorus that are the dominant constituents of most fertilisers. I also learnt a little about the use of lime to affect pH which can affect the release of nutrients to plants. The different soil types, from sandy to clay loams, were discussed in some detail along with the pros and cons of each. We learnt mainly that there were products we could buy which would solve many of what we thought were soil problems and that this was all we needed to grow good plants. As a fledgling organic gardener, I had deeply held misgivings about the use of chemical fixes, but it was years later that I learnt the facts behind my gut feelings.

It has been said that 'there are more organisms in a teaspoon of healthy soil than there are people in the world'. Given that we are teetering close to 8 billion people on this amazing planet of ours, that is an awful lot of life in a tiny amount of soil. Sometimes, when I am planting things in the garden, I hold the soil in the palm of my hand and peer closely, contemplating the assortment of living creatures I am holding, despite them being too minute for my eyes to register. These organisms range from the more well-known soil dwellers such as earthworms to microscopic creatures including bacteria and fungi. Each of these species plays a vital role in creating the phenomena of healthy, living soil, by ensuring that nutrients are recycled and made available to plant life, creating a good structure, and providing plenty of organic matter, enabling soils to capture and store water from rainfall and sequester carbon from the atmosphere.

Feet of clay

Becoming acquainted with your soil is an easy task. Start by looking at the soil in your garden or plot. Dig a bit of it up and examine it and try different areas to see if it varies at all. What does it look like? Is it dark coloured or pale? What does it feel like? Gardeners tend to classify soils as either sandy- or clay-based, as these are the opposite ends of the spectrum of the perfect loam, which hardly anyone has. Is it gritty to touch or soft and silky? Can you shape it into a ball or does it fall apart in your hands? All these things help you to define the type of soil you have to work with. All types of soil have their benefits and downsides. Clay soils hold nutrients and water well, but they tend to be waterlogged in the winter, slow to warm up and frequently bake as hard as concrete in a dry summer. Sandy soils, on the other hand, warm up quickly in spring, hardly ever get too soggy after heavy rain but they don't hold nutrients well, making plants smaller and less vigorous.

Often, we refer to soils as problematic, especially if we 'suffer' from heavy clay soils or even poor sandy ones. We see soils as being a barrier to overcome, yet another obstacle in our gardening journey. We bemoan our bad fortune and blame the soil for our lack of success in growing what we want in the garden and allotment. We may search for quick fixes, fertilisers and all manner of soil improvers yet, paradoxically, this is often the cause of our soils malfunctioning, resulting in unhealthy and disease-prone plants. We have failed to understand that soils can create and maintain fertility without our help and, in fact, it might be better to leave the gardener's interventions out of the loop in this finely tuned system. Our urge to dig and rotavate, remove plant cover to leave soils bare, spray weed killers, fungicides and insecticides have destroyed the finely tuned web of life, inherent within soil.

Healthy living soils are intrinsic to a well-balanced, functioning ecosystem. If you stop to think about it, soil is one of the main building blocks for all life on earth. Without soils, plant life would not exist and without plants, there would be very few other living things. Therefore, caring for soil should be one of the top priorities for anyone who works on the land, whether a large-scale farmer or the person who potters in a postage-stamp-sized garden; we are all equal in our responsibilities.

Most gardeners have heard of a 'friable loam', moist but well drained. It is a gardener's Shangri-la, a rare and desirable thing and we are told it is what all plants need to survive and thrive. In my experience, very few garden soils fall into that category! The next time you walk in a woodland, try taking a closer look at the soils which are found there below the tree canopy. Deciduous woodland is the best place to see what we are aiming for, rather than a conifer plantation. In woodland, no matter what the underlying soil type is, we will discover that there is a thick layer of dark coloured spongy soil, rich in organic matter and often teeming with tiny insects. If you smell it, it has the dark scent of mushrooms and sweet compost, it feels almost fluffy and sticky at the same time. This is soil which has been created by natural processes over decades, sometimes centuries, depending on the age of the woodland. Here, there has been no hand of the gardener or farmer to improve these soils, just a well-ordered group of specialist organisms which excel in the creation of topsoil. This is recycling and regeneration at its very best. Woodland soils are rich in organic matter and have a healthy mix of organisms contained within them, which enables trees, those long-lived giants of the natural world, to grow. Experts at ensuring that nothing is ever wasted, these soils and their inhabitants take the autumnal leaves, the fallen branches and the general detritus of life and death and make them into something new and accessible, for fresh plant life to emerge.

Permaculture principle: Produce no waste

This principle is a useful one to consider when it comes to soil and is fairly self-explanatory, in that it is based on the fact that there is no such thing as waste in nature; everything is reused or recycled in an endless loop. Many things we might consider to be waste can, in reality, be used in some way, such as leaves in the garden to make leaf mould to improve our soils or the use of cardboard packaging as a mulch to deter weeds. If we can't find a use for a product at the end of its life, we might want to ask ourselves if we can do without purchasing it in the first place. We can reduce the amount of stuff we buy or at least consider buying things which don't create a problem at the end of their useful lifespan. Moving away from single-use plastic items would be a great place to start. Learning to make compost is one of the best ways to rethink waste products as useful resources, which is central to being able to achieve a healthy, cyclical and self-nourishing environment.

For me, this also extends to my own aim not to waste my precious energy reserves and time on things which bring no benefits to either me or nature. This has been a difficult lesson for me to learn, for after all we are taught in modern society that we should measure our days by our productivity. All too often, we value things only by their financial worth, rather than whether they bring joy, healing or comfort to the proceedings. Nature has been a patient teacher throughout my exploration of my new identity as a co-operative assistant gardener and I now do my best to observe how best to improve any interventions I do make, and most importantly when to do nothing at all.

What can we learn from this about making our own soils healthier? Knowing that in nature, nothing is waste or superfluous to the system, we understand that everything can be broken down and reused in an enduring cycle of life. The key to this achievement is the biodiversity in our soils. We need those organisms whose entire role in life is to take the dead leaves, branches and even the bodies of other creatures and process them into a form that can be reused by plants in order to grow. The incredible web of subterranean life we call soil is something that I really wished I had realised and understood much earlier in my gardening adventures. Soil is a vast living ecosystem, complex and biodiverse but in miniature, right beneath our feet. Soil, which if it is in a healthy state, is self-regulating and capable of mining minerals from rocks, recycling nutrients and delivering those nutrients exactly where they are required, at the roots of plants. In fact, the co-operation and exchange between plants and many of the other organisms which live and survive within the soil is something we are only just beginning to comprehend.

The functioning system at the heart of a healthy soil is a food web, comprising a multitude of tiny organisms who live their lives within the soil, which are all co-dependent upon each other and the plants which grow there. Right at the bottom, underpinning all other interactions, are the bacteria and fungi. These are the organisms which create the nutrients a plant needs to grow. As these organisms die, they release nutrients, either to the creatures which eat them, or else back to the soil, in a form that plants can use.

Plants to the rescue again

Plants are the ones who appear to be in control of this system of soil and fertility and it seems they are capable of attracting the beneficial organisms that they need, to share their space. Let's face it, since they are immobile once growing, they have had to contrive ways to create the right conditions to attract soil life, which is then able to supply the plants with nutrients. As we know, plants are able to photosynthesise, which enables them to form carbohydrates, often in the form of sugar, from sunlight. I do realise that I am being rather simplistic here, but I don't want to spoil a good story by getting bogged down in the nitty gritty. These sugars are mainly used to grow leaves and stems, but a small amount is transported down to the plant's root system and is released into the soil, to act as edible lures for bacteria and fungi. These organisms, enticed to a particular location by the root's sugary gifts, provide the source of nutrients required by a plant to grow. In doing this, the plant is basically able to bring the nutrients it requires, right to where it needs it by bribing other organisms to come and co-operate with it. This two-way transfer of sugars from the plant and nutrients from fungi and bacteria are, at the most basic level, the way in which soils are fertile enough to support plant life. There are plenty of other actors on this stage too, from the sinister sounding Nematodes and Protozoa to the more jovially named Springtails and Microarthropods. Although generally these organisms are beneficial, not all of them are. It's a tough world down there and, just like in the jungle, there are plenty of larger predators prowling around to eat their unsuspecting prey. This of course also includes plants; as we well know, there are various soil dwellers who will happily make a meal of roots, shoots and leaves. A healthy soil will, however, work to keep populations of all microbes in balance, with the overall aim of creating a functioning ecosystem which will in turn grow healthy plants.

The more we learn more about the intricate connections that are occurring between the ecosystems beneath our feet, the more we realise that our attempts at bypassing nature to grow bigger and more plants, using fertilisers, pesticides and ploughing the soil, has broken the existing system which feeds us. Artificial fertilisers, consisting of concentrated salts, which when dissolved in water become available to plants as nutrients, are also highly toxic to many of the organisms in the soil. So, while it appears that we are doing good by applying them, as the plants we grow seem to thrive, we are only feeding the plants while destroying the soil biology, tying ourselves into a requirement to keep adding more artificial fertiliser in order to achieve the same results. This creates a dependency – almost like an addiction and just as harmful. The breakdown of the highly complex soil food web then allows some of the more resilient organisms to dominate, causing diseases to occur, which in turn require us to treat the ailing plants with yet more artificial sprays or additives. It becomes a downward spiral, where the only winners are the manufacturers of fertilisers and pesticides and their shareholders.

Given my own sad soil conditions, I realised that I needed to intervene if I was to achieve the thriving natural garden of my dreams. I had read an article about Korean natural farming, which utilises soils from local 'unimproved' ecosystems, in order to increase the number of indigenous microorganisms in depleted land. I decided to experiment, by bringing small amounts of soil and leaf mould from the edge of the ancient woodland which adjoins our property and adding this to the areas where I had planted trees and shrubs, in the hope of fast tracking the introduction of essential biology back to the soil. I also bought some soil additive in the form of a concentrated compost tea, which was also rich in different species of bacteria and fungi that allow soils to function as they were intended. I added this to the vegetable plot and the fruit trees. I'm pleased to report these additions have helped tremendously, with both the breakdown of organic matter and the creation of top soil, as well as the response by the plants, which have now begun to grow and thrive. I also make compost from kitchen waste, the manure from my chickens and sheep and anything I cut back from the garden – which isn't simply left on the ground – to add to my vegetable plot; this increases fertility by feeding the soil microorganisms, rather than the plants themselves. Composting is another form of alchemy, which I shall investigate more thoroughly later on.

Fungi

Fungi are an intrinsically important aspect to life on earth. Their presence in the soil is of particular importance, especially when it comes to plants. Plants and fungi have a close relationship, which we describe as being symbiotic, or mutually beneficial. They are so closely dependent on each other that sometimes it is difficult to separate them. That fungi are one of the main players in that biodiverse habitat beneath our feet comes as a shock to many people. We are, of course, familiar with their fruiting bodies, the toadstools which adorn our woodlands and fields during the autumn, but it is the microscopic mycelium which does the bulk of the work underground. You can think of mycelia as roots but they are just an alternative form of fungi and their threads are capable of covering miles within the soil.

There are a specific group of fungal organisms called *Mycorrhiza*, which attach themselves to the roots of plants in a co-operative endeavour. These fungi benefit from carbohydrates and sugars created by a plant during photosynthesis and the plants benefit from the vast and far-reaching network of soil fungi, which provides the plants with the nutrients it requires.

As gardeners we frequently think of fungi as being problematic, from mildews which attack our plants and stop them from thriving to honey fungus and other decay fungi which kill trees and other woody plants. In agriculture, where food crops are grown as monocultures in vast fields of just one species, fungi of course can be devastating. However, the use of fungicides as prophylactics, as a way of heading off problems before they even occur, also kills off the good fungi along with many of the other organisms. In a healthy ecosystem, no one species of fungi can dominate and cause problems. The wide range of different creatures present, such as bacteria, nematodes and other microorganisms, some of which eat fungi as their main food source, prevents any problems from becoming too severe.

Not only do bacteria and fungi play a major part in creating soil fertility, they also appear to connect plants together in order to create a kind of communication system. Fungi, especially, seem to be able to form links between plants of the same species, which allows them to not only send basic information to each other, such as the possibility of attack by another creature like aphids, but also to support each other by sharing nutrients. In a mature woodland, it has been discovered that trees are able to communicate basic information to each other about where best to link with their fungal partners in order to access nutrients, and also to support each other in a co-operative way. Therefore, if there are some trees living in less-than-ideal conditions, they do not suffer by being unable to access the same nutrients better-situated trees. That way, resources are shared within the tree species' community, allowing all to thrive and benefit. These fungal networks stretch for miles within soil and can move huge amounts of water and nutrients to where they are needed the most.

You can now see how fine a balance a healthy soil is: a self-regulating ecosystem, which thrives on being left alone. The role of plants within this system is equally important, as they provide much of the organic matter which feeds the system. Detrivores are organisms which break down the materials that plants leave behind when they shed leaves or die. These guys are the ultimate recyclers in nature, making sure nothing goes to waste and that the building blocks of life in its many facets are broken down into a form that other creatures can reuse.

The problems occur when we fail to understand how our interventions can be devastating to this fragile arrangement. The digging of soil on a regular basis, either with a spade or by using a rotovator, is one of the mistakes we can easily make. This disrupts the soil food web by breaking up the miles of fungal networks and therefore stopping the movement of nutrients within the soil. Initially, this can appear as a benefit to plants, causing a feeding frenzy by bacteria who feast on the dead fungi, releasing nutrients to plants. However, if this disruption is repeated, then the fungi don't have the chance to repair their networks, resulting in no food source for bacteria either, meaning the nutrients needed at the roots of plants often aren't available. Turning soils to expose them to the air and sunlight also kills many of the other soil microorganisms, which have evolved to exist in very specific conditions within the earth. Each has a particular role to play; they are the checks and controls on the system and their wide variety prevents any one of them being dominant and potentially upsetting the balance and causing detrimental plant diseases.

Invitations to celebrate the season

- This is the quietest of times in the garden and therefore I suggest that you give yourself permission to do nothing for a few weeks! Rather than fighting against the seasonal urge to hibernate, perhaps you can spend some time feeling warm and cosy, and allowing yourself to daydream about springtime instead. If you must do something, then collect some seasonal greenery to decorate your house for the Yule celebrations. Make wreaths, swags or simple bunches of twigs and evergreens to brighten your festivities.

- This time of year, with its very short days, makes it much easier to watch the sun rise. December dawns can often be incredibly beautiful and I encourage you to wrap up warm and go outside to watch the sun rise, especially on a crisp and frosty morning. Then come back inside for a nice hot cuppa.

- With the tradition of giving gifts at Christmas foremost in our minds, may I suggest that the nicest gifts are those which are made and not bought. If you don't feel that you have the time or necessary skills to bake a cake, sew a cushion cover, or create a small thing of beauty for someone, could you perhaps make your own greetings cards? You don't have to be a great artist … collage from magazines, potato printing or pressed leaves can all make interesting cards for friends and family. Allow yourself to play a little.

- If you have a personal wish list for potential festive gifts, why not consider upping your game in the composting of your vegetable waste? Can your family club together to buy (or make) a wormery, compost bin or Bokashi composting kit? Your garden soil and plants will love you if you do.

- After Yule is when you will find Seville oranges for sale in the greengrocers. Have you ever tried making marmalade? It is a fiddly and time-consuming task, but one in which I can happily lose myself for a few hours on a bleak and cold January day. Nothing tastes better than home-made preserves and the additional bonus is that your house will smell amazing too!

- If you are craving fresh crunchy salad at a time when your garden can only supply starchy root vegetables and hardy greens, try sprouting seeds. By growing mung beans, lentils, chickpeas or even marrowfat peas in a jar and keeping them in a warm place, they will grow into nutritious bean shoots for adding to salads and stirfries. Soak organic beans overnight, then drain them. Rinse twice a day and allow to drain again. In a few days they will provide delicious additions to your diet.

CHAPTER FOUR

It's still January!

New Year

January is my nemesis; I feel as though I have been locked into a battle with this month for most of my adult life. I can usually manage for about a week while congratulating myself on getting thus far with my sanity still intact, while knowing that by the end of the month I will be sobbing in a corner begging for it to end. I can forgive December, with its dwindling light and bone-chilling winds, because at least it promises fun and celebrations at the end of the darkness, but once these are out of the way, there is little to look forward to on the near horizon. Every year I tell myself that I will fully embrace the last vestiges of winter, these final few weeks before the extending days begin to stir the earth back into action again. Yet, despite my resolve, I become despondent, as day after day of dull and uninspirational hours parade slowly past, forcing me to stay indoors. The gloom sits heavily on me, like an endurance test, willing me to give in and move to the Caribbean or some such tropical paradise. I remind myself that I should use this time wisely to root deeply, restore and nourish myself and prepare for the eventual revival when spring takes back the reins. In the past, at the slightest hint of improving weather, I frequently became excitable and made stupid decisions to plant seeds, none of which ever thrived. Some emerged, encouraged out of their seedcases by central heating, only to discover that low light levels, draughty windowsills and fluctuating temperatures were not conducive to healthy growth. These days, I allow myself to take my cues from the changeable weather, making the most of being outdoors when the sun shines and using the more inclement hours for planning, designing and thinking about what I will do differently this year, all while sitting next to a woodburning stove with a cup of tea close to hand. My resolutions are all about doing less rather than more.

Deep in our hearts, we know the unspoken truth that spring will return. The seasonal wheel of life will turn again and we will lift ourselves out of the doldrums. Some I know busy themselves with spreadsheets and carefully hand-drawn plans, others bury themselves deep within the pages of the seed catalogues with ever-increasing wish lists. Yet while we distract ourselves from the stark realities of the winter garden, the earth is still hard at work. Like the trees, we must learn to bide our time. As the poet Rumi remarked: 'Don't think the garden loses its ecstasy in winter. It's quiet, but the roots are down there *riotous*.' This is nature's time to take the death and decay of the old year and harvest its energy for life to be reborn from its fertile remains. Inspired by this thought, I spread compost from my bins on the vegetable plots, even though it doesn't yet resemble the perfect crumbly stuff of my dreams. It will just as happily break down into this utopian state of affairs in situ and it allows me to feel that I am doing something useful on sunny days. By the time I am ready to begin sowing seed and planting out again, the soil's inhabitants will have decomposed, processed and been nourished by these additions and my vegetable plants will stand a good chance of success.

It's an excessively January day. I feel depleted and sluggish, so I give myself permission to stay indoors. I am comforted by the fact that nature doesn't fight against the winter days, attempting to carry on as though it was still summer, and that this is still a time of rest, before the renewal. I let my actions echo the quiet persistence of the trees, biding their time with an unyielding trust that spring will return. The clouds hang low, heavy and sludgy grey, matching my low mood. It is relatively mild though for the time of year and I must remind myself that winter lurks far longer in these northern hills, so now is not the time to be too optimistic and start sowing vegetable seeds just yet. The onion seed can wait until after Imbolc, when I might have more motivation. Despite this, the birds seem busy with their preparations for the coming season, the robins and wrens being the first birds to start and end the day with a song.

I decide to sharpen and oil my secateurs ready to begin winter pruning once the weather improves. I have a young apple orchard, which I planted in my first winter here in the garden, and a couple of pear trees that I am training as espaliers on the south-facing wall at the end of the house. I chose the apples partly for their flavours, although some I chose simply because I loved their names: Peasegood Nonsuch, Ashmeads Kernel, Egremont Russet and Ribston Pippin; their names sound like chanted incantations or spells, curious and mystical, all clearly with stories to tell. I book myself in with gardening customers for the annual rose prune too, keeping my fingers crossed for a mild day, as this can be a brutally cold job if the wind is blowing from the north. The sun emerges briefly beneath the blanket of cloud as it sinks into the horizon, so I pull on my coat and wellies for a last wander around with the dogs. I search the borders for signs of life and I'm delighted to discover the first green snouts of bulbs emerging from the cold ground. The days are lengthening visibly now and I give the hens their last meal at half past four and shut down the coop, just as the dusk begins to darken the skies and the rooks fly to their roosting trees.

Soil and health

Another excellent reason to take care of soil is that healthy soils also contain microorganisms which are beneficial to our health, specifically our gut microbiome. There seems to be an increasing amount of evidence which points to the fact that soil health leads directly to gut health and therefore better human health, both physical and mental. There are huge numbers of microbes, consisting of mainly bacteria, which exist within our gastro-intestinal tract. This community of microbes, or microbiota, directly affects our digestion, metabolism, immune system and mental states. While our microbiota is largely inherited from our mothers at birth, environmental factors such as diet, drugs or other chemical exposure and our physical interactions with the natural world play a greater part in determining the range of microbes we host. We are learning that a healthy gut microbiome is essential to human health and that the diversity of these populations has declined in recent years, due to our modern lifestyles and the industrialisation of our food supply. This has led to a rise in obesity, auto-immune diseases and declines in mental health, among other things. A species-rich and diverse gut ecosystem is more likely to be able to cope with environmental factors, avoiding ill health and reversing the damage caused by our stressful lifestyles and exposure to environmental toxins. Clearly, we are not only part of nature, but we are indeed nature. As human beings, we are host to a wide range of microbes, which leads me to wonder if we are in fact ecosystems ourselves.

Research has discovered that healthy soils contain 100 trillion different microbes, approximately the same number as the population within our guts. Pre-industrial communities frequently were in much closer contact with the soil due to more people working the land. As people moved to urban settings, this changed. We need to consider that our food comes from the soil, either directly as vegetables and fruit or indirectly via animals and that the two microbiomes of soil and gut are intrinsically linked. While this branch of scientific enquiry is still very much in its infancy, there are already signs that the failing health of soils, due to industrial processes and use of artificial fertilisers and pesticides, is mirrored in our own deteriorating health and well-being, especially with the rise of auto-immune disorders, as I know all too well. There is evidence that there is even some form of communication between the microbiome in soil and our own cells, leading to positive changes in nutrient levels in food plants. As unlikely as this might seem, there is an urgent need to discover more about our personal microbe communities, how our health is directly affected by them and how we can improve soil health by regenerative practices to restore the soil ecosystem in order to increase the nutrient density of the food we eat.

You don't have to be a vegetable grower – or even someone suffering from an auto-immune disorder – to be concerned about soil health and how it affects you. Your everyday interactions with the soil, even if that just means pulling up the occasional weed or walking barefoot across your lawn, can be beneficial to your health, just by physical contact with the soil's ecosystem. It seems there is an ancient relationship between the bacteria in our bodies and those in the soil. In Finland, scientists experimented by putting a 'forest floor' in children's school playgrounds to see if this made any difference to their health and immune systems. The play areas were transformed by bringing in soil and plants from a nearby wild area. The researchers installed a patch of meadow, shrubs and plants from the woodland and the children had the chance to care for plants in raised planters. Not surprisingly, it turned out that children who had the chance to play in an environment with natural soils and vegetation had higher levels of friendly bacteria living on their skin, and their immune systems were working better than children who only had access to tarmac to play on. These children with the introduced forest floor had the same diversity of healthy gut microbes as children who are able to visit and play in actual forests on a daily basis. This phenomenon is known as the 'biodiversity hypothesis' which suggests that our immunity and our overall health is positively impacted by our exposure to an environment rich in living things. Scientists have even identified a particular bacterium called *Mycobacterium vaccae* which can stimulate serotonin, that feel-good chemical in our brains. By being in contact with these soil-based bacteria, it can make us feel happier, more vital and less stressed, almost as if we were taking anti-depressants. Spending time in the garden getting your hands dirty might be the boost you need if you are feeling low for any reason. It's amazing that soils can be such conduits for positive change in our lives.

Permaculture principle: Obtain a yield

This principle suggests that we should focus our energies and time on ensuring that we gain a benefit from any work we carry out. That yield can be a simple and tangible one such as cut flowers for the house, herbs for cooking with, more birds in the garden. Alternatively, a more abstract but no less valuable yield, for instance, is a positive boost to our mental health by having a verdant and beautiful outdoor space near to our home, or a peaceful place to sit and find sanctuary. This principle ensures that we can value a wide range of outcomes from our interactions with nature, not just the monetary value assigned to things. Personally, I believe that the best things in life are free, so creating a garden where you are able to watch the sun rise or set, appreciate the form and beauty of chosen plants and flowers, or simply having a bolt hole to escape to are worth far more than financial value of a pretty garden or a productive vegetable plot.

Growing vegetables, however, is the one thing which I find to be the most satisfying of garden tasks. I think I have always been fascinated by the ability to grow food so close to hand. My paternal grandparents were excellent role models for me, as my grandpa was an incredible vegetable grower and he first introduced me to the delights of eating a ripe tomato fresh off the vine, still warm from the sun and bursting with sweet juices. I'm not sure I really stood a chance after that and it was only a matter of time before I had my own herb garden at home and I started to grow radishes and carrots between my parent's rosebushes. I think I was around 6 years old at this time. Growing vegetables teaches you to be a more inventive cook as well, as you learn to deal with seasonality and gluts. In my early twenties, when I was unemployed, I learnt to be incredibly creative with courgettes and runner beans one summer, when that was my staple dietary input.

While I still frequently struggle with my personal energy reserves, the growing of vegetables in order to provide organic, fresh seasonal food for myself is now a non-negotiable aspect of my lifestyle. Eating food which is so nutrient dense and barely a few minutes old between harvesting, cooking and eating, is, I believe, one of the contributing factors to my recovery from ill health. While I realise that having sufficient land to grow vegetables is a huge privilege and one denied to many people, everyone can grow micro-greens on the windowsill or a pot of salad leaves in the back yard or on the balcony. If we all could learn to provide even a tiny amount of the food that we consume, we might learn to have a better understanding of what fuels us and that growing our own food adds value to our lives well beyond the basic financial savings we might make.

We have had a week of those January days which are unremarkable in their demeanour, unlovable and brooding, their sulky presence wearing you down. Like an unwanted house guest, I have learnt to tolerate them, suffering in silence and ignoring them as best I can. I am not at my best at this time of year and it has taken me years to realise that instead of pushing through and attempting life as normal, I actually do much better when I succumb to the urge to hibernate next to the fire. I aim to emulate nature and allow myself some down-time, where I can plan, plot and dream. Just as nature becomes dormant in winter, building up reserves and ensuring that the roots are strong and deep enough to weather the winter storms, before it all begins again as the wheel turns, I go to bed early, sleep more than usual and use the time to bake, read, do crafts and, in my case, do garden designs for people, as I do still need to work. I find design to be an excellent distraction from what it happening outside the window, as I always begin the design process with fifteen minutes meditation and visualisation, when I can transport myself to sunnier days, filled with flowers.

On those precious winter days, when the sun does shine, I always try to get outside for even just a short while. Wrapped up warm with scarf, hat and gloves, I walk around the garden, admiring the winter bones of the trees and shrubs and the skeletal remains of summer's blooms. This is the time when you can see the garden more clearly, without the distraction of bright colours, and you can prune any unwanted growth to make way for the new, as well as planning for any new planting that might suggest itself. It is in the winter when I really understand the benefit of evergreen shrubs and the ways in which we can add colour to a winter border without resorting to trays of winter pansies. I am a huge fan of the dogwoods with their colourful stems of scarlet and I like to combine these with early flowering bulbs, such as snowdrops, to make a little display of interest, all the better if it can be viewed through the window from the house. I will soon be cutting back my dogwoods to keep the stems bright and colourful; it also helps to keep them a manageable size. I use the cut stems in floral arrangements in the house or occasionally I weave small baskets and platters from them, although the colour fades eventually, once they dry.

Pruning

Winter is a traditional time to carry out any necessary pruning of woody plants, while the plants are dormant. Pruning can be a thorny and divisive subject, and is a skill which is now becoming lost, since many gardeners now use mechanised hedge trimmers, which can turn everything into an amorphous blob shape. To be perfectly honest, most shrubs and trees don't actually need pruning at all. They won't die if we don't prune them and this bit of a gardener's role definitely falls into the category of unnecessary but perhaps nice-to-do. Incidentally, the pruning of flowering shrubs with a hedge trimmer to make them look 'tidy' is the main cause of lack of flowering. Many shrubs flower on the previous year's growth, so if this is cut away at the end of the growing season, then it is unlikely to encourage a good show of flowers. Try to accept a more natural shape, perhaps just thinning out by removing a few old stems at ground level every year instead.

The pruning of fruit trees, particularly apples, has a long history of being carried out after the Yule festivities, with the celebration of Wassailing. Wassailing was a time when the community would come together to do the winter pruning, toast the health of the trees with a glass of mulled cider, with a tiny amount to be poured around the tree's roots, and an almighty noise was created with the banging of pots, pans, drums and whistles. The voices of everyone singing wassail songs were added encouragement to frighten away any bad spirits that might be lurking in the orchard. You don't need a good or tuneful singing voice to be an expert in wassailing!

I love apples, I have a very long history with them. When I started my first head gardener role, there were three orchards in the walled garden and I had very little experience of fruit growing. This is the sort of thing which is no longer taught in colleges, so I bought books to help me learn, as this was in those dim and distant days before YouTube arrived on the scene.

I was helped by an older lady called Bobby, a member of a stalwart group of people known as the Northern Fruit Group. She had long grey hair, infinite patience to teach me her pruning knowledge and an amazing singing voice. I have extremely fond memories of cold winter days in that garden, as we stood discussing the form and function of each particular tree, while we carefully removed crossing and unwanted branches, leaving piles of twiggy brash laying around, her operatic voice echoing from the old stone walls as the dusk closed around us at the end of the day and the mist rose from the ground.

The great untangling

Pruning is one of those tasks which can feel quite daunting. With so many books illustrated with before and after photos, diagrams with the branches to remove marked in red, it's no wonder that folks get anxious. It's the same when dealing with anything that appears complicated. The first reaction is panic: where to begin. Comparing what you have to deal with, to another's situation is always likely to cause problems. It's the same with difficult problems in life; it's often hard to make the first move and the very thought of it can make us anxious and unempowered. An hour of careful pruning in the garden has often allowed me the time and space to come to a decision when I have been feeling uncertain.

I am never entirely sure as to how much pruning we should be aiming to do in a natural garden, after all there is little in the way of pruning carried out in nature. Perhaps this is where we go wrong. On the whole, shrubs and trees are not going to be adversely affected if we simply leave them alone to grow as nature intended. Generally, I find that we feel the need to cut things back purely because things have outgrown the space that we had allocated for them. It is at this point that I feel we need to challenge our own perceptions of what it means to be a gardener and question carefully why we feel we need to do anything. Perhaps we just want to cut away a few dead branches in the middle of a shrub. After all, this is something which would happen naturally, as if a branch was dead it would eventually fall and rot on the ground, so maybe we are simply speeding up that process. Trimming growth back from paths or 'lifting the skirts' of low-growing branches can enable us to access the garden without getting wet, or grow a colourful puddle of spring-flowering bulbs underneath an established shrub; as such, I feel that this falls into the category of playful creativity rather than strict control.

We often have it in our heads that flowering shrubs flower and often fruit better if we prune them. It is rare that this is the case. In some respects, the action of browsing wild animals nibbling at the end of a few tasty branches might encourage a shrub to produce more flowers. This might trigger something which makes the plant feel under threat and in need of producing seed as a way of ensuring its survival. However, it is usually due to aesthetic considerations that we undertake pruning, which isn't always a bad thing, but I reiterate that we should question this carefully before we begin. I know that many people think that trees require pruning on a regular basis to keep them safe and healthy, while the fact of the matter is that the reverse of this is true. Trees generally grow far better if they are left unpruned, as they have developed structures and systems which function perfectly well without the need for limbs being lopped off. Leaving open cut wounds on trees leaves them open to fungal and bacterial infections and subsequent decay which can significantly shorten their lifespan.

Mindful pruning

As with all things in the garden and in life, the best place to start is by taking a few deep breaths. Standing in front of the plant you want to prune, take time to view it properly and have an idea in your head what it is you want to achieve. Maybe you don't yet know what you want to achieve, but sometimes just deciding to make a start, with a pair of secateurs in hand and preferably the sun on our back, can be enough to set us on our way. Sometimes that's all it takes to start to snip away at the things that no longer serve a purpose and just get in the way. Things that have become redundant and are no longer needed can be removed to make space for new growth. In gardening we refer to these as the three Ds: dead, dying and diseased; these branches are always the first to be removed. There is no benefit in retaining them and they often over-complicate the structure of the plant, preventing us from seeing what we need to do to create a better structure. In life, I rather like to consider them as the depressing, the (out) dated and the damaging – behaviours or belongings which we continue to keep despite the fact that they no longer need to be part of our lives and, as in gardening, these things can cloud our views of the path ahead or entangle us to the extent that we feel unable to move forward.

As with most things, I find that it's the thought of starting which is so hard … as long as you realise that you're unlikely to kill either the plant or yourself, approaching a new task with curiosity and a sense of adventure is the best way forward. Intend to work with the smallest actions you can get away with to begin. You might well feel like being brutal later on, but do start small, as little changes can still produce big results.

Take your time, work slowly. Take only a little bit at a time. Rushing into things tends to lead to mistakes. Start with the easy stuff, the bits that are easy to recognise, the bits that are dead or dying or blatantly unhealthy. Prune out these bits to begin. Now, what do you have left? Has that made things any easier? Seeking clarity in a situation should be a thoughtful process. I personally like to prune without wearing gloves, even if I am working with roses. I find that the extra care I need to take to avoid ripping my skin on the thorns, forces me to take a more considered approach to the task. I can't honestly say that I end the day without at least a few scratches but, generally, both the roses and myself benefit from a slower process.

The next move is to see if you can identify anything which is developing in the wrong direction. Is this using up a lot of energy and growing towards a brick wall or interfering with something you want to hang on to? Perhaps these crossing branches, which rub against each other and cause friction can be trained to develop differently. Or else is it worth just selecting one of them and completely removing the other, in order to bring a clearer structure into being? Consider these different options and try to follow them through different scenarios to see which might best suit the situation.

Aim for a simple structure, with just a few strong shoots. This teaches us not to try to do too much. Focus your energies on what you need. Don't aim to put your energies into too many things all at once. This often leads to burnout and leaves complexity and tangles in its wake. Too many growing shoots left on one plant depletes all of them, preventing fruits from developing and ripening, or buds from forming for next year.

What about then concentrating on the things that have already produced what you needed them too. Do you still need them? Will they come in use again? Can they be taken away now to make room for something new and more productive? Is it time for them to be added to the compost bin, where they can break down and be recycled into something useful again?

Feel free to take your time over this. Make sure that you stop what you are doing and stand back from time to time to admire your work. This gives you a different viewpoint and perspective, which of course works for all sorts of things, not just pruning. Viewing either a tangled-up shrub or personal dilemma from lots of angles enables you to see different ways of approaching a problem. Try to stand back and assess; once you have removed some of the things you have decided you no longer need, ask if it has made things clearer. Does it look better yet? Can you see now what it is you are trying to achieve? I always suggest that a third of the time you spend pruning should be spent looking and thinking, rather than sawing or snipping, where sometimes it can lead to getting carried away in your enthusiasm to do rather too much. The old adage is that once pruned you can't put something back again, so that viewing time is essential and all the better if you can do it with a cup of steaming hot tea or coffee, as a reward for all your hard work and determination.

Invitations to celebrate the season

- To get through the month of January, I have to start to imagine that spring is on its way, even though I know in my heart there will be plenty of weeks of rubbish weather yet to come. I dig out my box of seeds and look through them, making a list of what I might need to buy for the upcoming growing season. While it's far too early to be starting anything off yet, especially up here on these northern hills, I like to have the opportunity to dream and plan a little.

- A couple of weeks into January and my mind turns to pruning. I have a small number of customers to whom I always pay a visit in order to prune and train, either their fruit or roses. I will only do this on those rare sunny days when it's not too windy, so I usually offer a range of possible dates and I choose the best days for me to wrap up warm and do some untangling. If you're unsure where to begin with pruning, why not check out some videos on YouTube? Watch different people's techniques and be aware that there is never just only one way to do something in the garden. Maybe you can come up with something suitable for your own particular situation?

- January can be a good time to mulch beds and borders. Don't worry if your compost isn't perfect. Roughly made compost is just as good and often rots down more quickly as a layer on top of the soil than it does in the compost bin. The rest of the natural world may seem to be sleeping, but the soil organisms are still busy at work beneath our feet and would appreciate some love and attention.

- Keep feeding the birds. It's a hungry time of year and a few sunflower seeds can make all the difference. Perhaps you can grow some of your own sunflowers next year and

51

save the seed for feeding the birds, to save a bit of money? Don't forget that water is essential too so especially on frosty days, try to supply a source of water throughout the day. Don't forget that seeing birds in the garden is one of the easiest ways to feel happier!

- Dig up a small clump of snowdrops, as soon as their green snouts appear, and pot them into a small terracotta pot. Put moss around the top and bring them into the house. Placed on a shady windowsill and kept well-watered, they will come into flower much earlier than in the garden and evoke a sense of spring cheer. They have a very delicate scent, which often goes unnoticed in the garden. Place the pot where you can stop and inhale their fragrance from time to time. Once they have finished flowering, return them to the garden.

CHAPTER FIVE

Imbolc

Six weeks after the winter solstice, on 1st February, we celebrate the festival of Imbolc, which heralds the end of winter's grip on the land. I bring a small terracotta pot of snowdrops into the house, which I lifted from the garden in order to force them into flower early. I cut twigs from the willows I have planted in the wetter parts of the garden and place them in vases of water. I have learnt to love willow, since it grows so well in the soggy land around the stream which runs at the back of the house. I have one which has pink catkins, a Japanese variety called 'Mount Aso' which willingly bursts into bud within a few hours of bringing it into the warm kitchen. I admire its soft candyfloss-coloured buds and look forward to its appearance out in the garden. The word Imbolc is said to mean ewes' milk and it refers to that stage of pregnancy in sheep where ewes begin to produce milk in readiness for lambing; the sheep farmers in my part of the moors refer, somewhat less romantically, to their ewes as 'bagging up'.

It is the cusp of the growing season; buds are beginning to swell and the snouts of spring bulbs are peeking out of the surface of the still cold earth. This time of year, after months of cold dark days, I am relishing the slightly longer days, although it feels premature to be thinking of spring. One of the first signals that spring might be on the way are the noises made by the frogs in my tiny wildlife pond in order to attract a mate, usually heard on a late February evening, just as the sun slips below the horizon; it never fails to bring a smile to my face. Soon after, those first gelatinous blobs of life appear, as the frogspawn begins to make a presence in the shallows and you can be sure that winter's end is in sight at last.

It was a bright morning, crisp underfoot with puddles frozen hard, when I went out to feed the hens their corn. By ten o'clock, it had clouded over and the wind was sucking at the chimneys making the fires roar. I am weary of winter by now, these days of grey are unremarkable, unloved and brooding, their sulky presence wears me down. Wet and squally showers arrived, driven in by westerly gales, stripping away the cobwebs of winter's dormancy in preparation for the changing of seasons. The land sleeps, hunkered down, while winter still holds sway. Yet in the sheltered nooks and crannies of the garden, green shoots of new life emerge, pale snowdrops raise their heads and hazel catkins sway in anticipation of better days. In the woods, the woodpeckers drum on hollow trees, setting the rhythm for the swell and thrust of imminent growth, a drum roll for winter's departure from the main stage.

Permaculture principle: Apply self-regulation and feedback

This permaculture principle is a reminder to check in from time to time to see what has worked well and what hasn't succeeded. It suggests that we can learn from our mistakes and change course if needs be. Nothing needs to be set in stone; being adaptable to all things in life is a good lesson to learn. This is something that I frequently do, as plants can be a fickle bunch and, despite everything, I often have to admit defeat and move plants around in the garden in the hope of finding a place where they will thrive rather than struggle to survive. One of my friends calls this process 'moving the ornaments about on the mantlepiece'. If you take the time to carefully observe a plant, it will tell you if it is happy or not. Yellowing leaves, lack of growth in spring, a tendency to suffer from pests and diseases are all symptoms that a plant is not thriving as well as it should be.

This has been an important lesson for me to learn on a purely personal basis too. Learning to listen to my body is not something I had previously done, apart from the occasional stomach rumble reminding me to eat something, or an aching back suggesting that I take a break from weeding. I now try to check in with myself at least a few times a day and ask myself how I feel and what do I need. I also prefer to do this while I am outside in the garden in what I now consider to be my preferred natural habitat. I am easily distracted when in the house by the multitude of tasks which clamour for my attention, even if all I do is then ignore them. These days, I try to take the time to stop, listen to what is happening in nature firstly and then turn my attention to myself.

It can be hard sometimes when a project you have been involved in fails to succeed and you have to admit defeat and try again in a different place. There are many areas in my garden which I began to plant things in during my early days here. Several of them have returned to nature, as I discovered that trying to cultivate ground which was thick with invasive couch grass was always going to be a lot of effort. In one case, the perennials I originally planted have found a way to co-exist with the grass and I have a rather lovely non-native meadow of hardy *Geraniums*, *Hellebores*, snowdrops and perennial cornflower (*Centaurea montana*). I have carefully dug out the cyclamen I had brought from my mother's garden and moved them into an area where they can grow without competition.

It's mid-February, late winter and I am sheltering in the greenhouse. The mild sunny days earlier in the month had lifted my spirits enough to think that spring was just around the corner. As ever, I knew in my heart that it was far too early and just as the blackthorn blossom began to make an appearance in the hedgerows, the winter returned, as it always does. The rain – or is it sleet? – is rattling like artillery on the glass. Lined up on the bench is a selection of seed packets, some flowers, some vegetables. Despite the cold and damp, I am stirred to action, to begin the annual ritual of sowing seed. Perhaps it's something primeval, a half-remembered urge to be involved in the age-old process of life and renewal. It feels as though a force is acting on me, spring always affects me in that way. Today, though, winter still has a strong grip, not yet ready to relinquish its power and let go. I plant seeds anyway, knowing that spring will follow winter, as it does every year. There is certainty in these cycles, something we can rely on. There is comfort in routine, the slow seasonal shift, coming around full circle, trundling on like an old wooden cart. The track it follows might be rutted and bumpy, but the cart continues, the wheels turning, winter into spring and summer into autumn. Always going forwards, each season a brand-new experience.

Observing the cycle of the seasons reminds us that change is normal. In our modern society, we are creatures of habit and we seek the comfort of routine and certainty, rather than the chaos of not knowing. The garden teaches us that there is pleasure to be had in these more liminal spaces, between the seasons. We prepare ourselves by sowing seeds, our good intentions for a new season inherent in each one we plant. A seed needs both darkness and light in order to grow, and it appears that we do too. Learning to embrace the dark, more challenging times and accepting them as being as essential to our growth as the bright, joyful days, has been an important lesson for me to learn.

While mindlessly scrolling through social media feeds, I realise that Valentine's Day has become the time when the keenest of vegetable gardeners begin to sow their seeds for those slower-growing, heat-loving plants, such as chillies, aubergines and tomatoes. I am suddenly heartened that what had become just another overtly commercial day of the celebration of love, is now being hijacked by those of us who love growing, gardening and raising our own plants. The sowing of seeds of love embodies a profoundly better celebration of the day, rather than the consumption of imported flowers, soaked in toxins and using valuable resources, which could be better used to feed people. This now is a celebration I can really get behind.

Seed sowing

Seed sowing is a miraculous process, and one I never tire of experiencing. Anyone who has ever sown a few seeds in the soil and had them emerge and grow into plants, surely cannot deny the influence of magic in that accomplishment. There is something very life affirming about sowing seed. That tiny organic object has the innate ability, with a little help, to grow into something beautiful and useful. Soil, water and sunshine are all it takes to complete the transformation. From commonplace weeds to towering trees, they all started life as seeds. I marvel at the potential of seeds, that magical metamorphosis from pip to plant.

Of course, as gardeners, we can help this process along the way. We nurture the miracle by ensuring it has the very best start in life: Shop-bought compost, a nice clean seed tray, sufficient heat, light and moisture. Cosseted like spoilt children, we bestow our hopes on to them. While some might feel that growing plants from seed is too slow a journey, I like to think that the patience this can teach us is a treasure to be nurtured. Nature moves in time spans different to our own; the life of trees span several of our generations and teach us that continuity and rootedness in place is something to be grateful for. It acts as a reminder that our simple tasks of sowing, growing and harvesting are humble pursuits that have stood the test of time. Working with our backs to the sun and our hands in the earth, we take part in rituals and responsibilities which have passed down through many generations of gardeners and germinations of seed.

Every year, I always have the same surge of excitement when I see the first green shoots of growth. I begin the year during those dismal, dark days in January, when it's hard to even imagine spring, by rummaging through my box of seed packets and picking out a few select seeds which will grow, even in these inconceivably difficult few weeks. Chillies take ages to germinate and therefore need to be started early and I use a heated propagator to get them going. Happy to grow on a sunny windowsill, their plucky growth against the odds feels like heralds of spring, all the more welcome on these dull days.

Now consider your role in this, how does it feel? To me it seems as though I am planting seeds of hope and optimism. Looking at those tiny packets of plant potential. Are the seeds as you imagined they would look? What size are they? Some are so tiny they resemble dust, like poppy seed or foxglove, others are much more substantial and sturdy. Some seeds are so delicate that they make me feel as though I have chubby chipolatas for fingers and I struggle to sow them thinly enough. Others are so beautiful in their own right, I spend quite a bit of time admiring them … runner beans, for example, are extraordinarily handsome, with their delicate pink background, mottled all over in chocolate brown freckles, although I might add that these are usually the latest seeds to be planted, as I rarely start them before Beltane.

Sinking my hands into the compost, I feel at once calmer and more grounded. How does that compost feel? Is it suitable for the seeds you are sowing – not too coarse in texture or too dry and dusty? Is there anything you can do to make a more satisfactory seedbed? I like to buy peat-free and organic compost. Peat-free is always preferable, as peat bogs are a particularly special and fragile ecosystem and it would be sacrilege to damage such a rare and delicate environment in the pursuit of creating a natural garden. You can even just sow in ordinary garden soil so it doesn't have to cost too much money. The tinier the seeds, the finer the compost needs to be. If the compost appears too coarse, then use a sieve to cover the seed with finer material. The larger bits you remove can be used in the bottom of a pot to improve drainage.

Ensuring that the seeds are planted at the correct depth is important. Be mindful to avoid burying them too deeply. You don't want them to have to struggle to reach the light they require in order to become strong healthy seedlings. Don't make life more difficult for them – your role here is as an enabler. Never forget that nature can do this all by herself!

What are you sowing – is it food or flowers? Do you know where in your garden these young plants will be growing? Are you able to imagine those plants when they are full size providing you with delicious crops or delighting you with beautiful blooms, while the bees explore what they have to offer? It is great to have all this in mind when sowing, but I also fall into the category of someone who 'probably' buys too many seeds every spring, without a thought of where they will end up. Please don't worry, if this is you. Gardeners will always find a way, even if it means that all your friends and neighbours are given seedlings in pots because you have too many. A gift of a pot of seedlings is a thoughtful one.

Intent

Sowing intentions while sowing seeds is a very potent tool for change in your life. There is something about spring and its promise of new beginnings after the long struggle through the winter months. Can you harness this energy? You need to be aware of it first … notice how quickly things change in the springtime. Every day brings a new revelation: more leaves appearing in the trees; tiny flowers popping up from bare soil; and a flurry of activity from flocks of birds as they prepare to claim their territory, build nests and raise their young.

It was while seed sowing that I made the decision to do everything within my abilities to turn around my ill health and investigate what small steps I needed to take to improve my life. I began by pledging to grow and eat as much of my own food as possible and although I am not self-sufficient by any degree, I do manage to supply my vegetable needs for a sizeable part of the year. Making the effort to cook from scratch using whatever is available in the garden or the freezer has made me into a more adventurous cook and the positive effect on my health has been remarkable.

I like to think that when I am growing vegetables from seed that I can reduce my dependence on industrial agriculture and the associated food miles. Knowing that I can grow tasty vegetables to supplement the food I buy from the shops makes me very proud. The taste of home-grown vegetables and herbs is better than anything money can buy. While not everybody has the space to be fully or even partially self-sufficient, the simple act of growing a few pots of herbs or salad leaves can feel like a revolutionary act in a world where our worth is often measured in our ability to consume and spend money. That small act of self-reliance can be surprisingly empowering.

Even growing flowers from seed is a wonderful experience. Being able to pick a bunch of flowers from your own garden is a deeply satisfying weekly ritual for me during the summer months. Sitting down with a cup of coffee next to a flower border and seeing the bees busy collecting pollen and nectar from flowers you have grown is a satisfying moment. Watching those first flashes of growth in springtime feels like a flow of optimism after a long and depressing winter. Deciding to improve your garden, by growing something from seed, is a very powerful commitment. Nurturing that seed by providing it with what it needs to grow can remind you that while changes might be small, simple daily tasks can make a huge difference over a long period.

Checking on the growth of young seedlings every day reminds us to check in with ourselves too. Is there anything we can do to make us grow well? More water, more sunshine, the perfect environment where we can fulfil our full potential? Can we give ourselves the same amount of care that we give to our seedlings? Most importantly, give yourself praise for learning to communicate on a deeper level with nature, because this is what we do when we plant seeds. Choosing to grow seeds, which are the building blocks of plant life, and invite them into your garden is a simple choice that can bring great pleasure.

Growing plants from seed also ensures that biodiversity isn't lost. As we have already explored, nature works best with a variety of all species and that reducing that choice is a move towards uniformity and monoculture. A potential recipe for disaster, especially given our changing climate and the emergence of new diseases and the spread of pests into new areas. Over time, we have saved and engineered seed to provide us with what seems like an almost bewildering choice, although in reality the number of varieties of flowers and especially vegetables available to buy has decreased rapidly over the last few decades. In the case of commercial food crops, it has been estimated that this loss of diversity is in the region of 90 per cent. This is a sad loss of some lovely old heirloom varieties and to me feels short-sighted in its approach.

It's late February and I walk into the room that I use as an office and realise that it smells of things growing. I have set up my heated propagator on a small coffee table in there and it is so full of pots, I have two trays of early peas balanced on top of the cover, to make use of any rising heat. The smell is a subtle yet indescribable scent, similar to the scent of damp earth yet with more complex green, sappy notes complementing the earthiness. I realise this is the smell that I am waiting for outside. Every morning when I walk the dogs up the track, to stretch our collective legs, I am very aware of the seasonal changes and as yet the air still definitely smells of winter, crisp and cold with little nuance or complexity. I have noticed the first tentative song of the skylarks on our neighbour's fields though, and this feels like another turning point in the year, even though it does seem that spring has decided to take the scenic route. Last night, I noticed that after the rain I could detect the smell of petrichor, the smell of wet soil after rain, something which I rarely notice through the winter months. I wonder if this means that the soil-based organisms are beginning to awaken, if indeed they ever do sleep. I remind myself to be patient and continue to conserve my energy before the rush of growth and activity that will arrive with the grand entrance of spring.

The type of seed that you choose to grow is important. There are several types of seeds available which produce hybrids, bred especially by seed companies for bigger and better plants, brighter flowers, uniformity of growth. These are called F1 hybrids, which means that they have been produced by crossing two different parent plants. They may seem as though they offer the gardener something better as, in the short term, the plants are more vigorous and offer greater yields with more uniformity, although if we look a little closer, we see that this might not always be to our advantage. Many F1 hybrids, particularly in the example of vegetables, were bred by seed companies for farmers and market gardeners who usually want to crop their harvest all in one go. This trait is of little benefit to the home grower, however, as it tends to result in gluts of crops, which then require quite a bit of time and effort to process and preserve, otherwise the excess we are unable to eat goes to waste. From the perspective of flowers, many of the F1 hybrids are likely to produce 'fancy' blooms, often double-flowered varieties, many of which are sterile. Their sterility means that they bloom for longer, but they offer no benefit to insects, as they frequently do not produce nectar and pollen in any quantity and the 'doubling' of individual flowers means that even if there is something for the insects, they are unable to access it, due to the complexity of the flower structure.

The month of March arrived sullenly, foggy and grey. I guess this must count as coming in like a lamb, rather than a lion, and although the gloom pervaded my bones, the birdsong was insistent in its declaration that spring was coming. The anticipation is such that it feels as though we will be plunged into spring any moment, yet in reality the transition from winter to spring is a much gentler, if bumpy slide. By March, the temperatures are steadily improving, yet day to day the fluctuations can be immense, even more so if the wind is blowing. Observing the change of seasons is a good way to learn about microclimate within a garden. At that most critical of times, at the cusp of growth, a warm and sheltered niche can give you two weeks or more advantage over a more exposed or shaded spot. If you are growing vegetables, or early flowering beauties, such as camellias or hellebores, the difference in microclimates around your garden can inform you as to the best places to plant things.

I watch the birds on the feeders and decide that the goldfinches and the cock pheasant are in cahoots. The finches are messy eaters, scattering sunflower seeds with abandon, while the pheasant, looking dapper in his seasonal finery, hoovers up the droppings, clucking and muttering in his appreciation. I'm not entirely sure what the goldfinch gets from this deal, but the arrangement seems to work well. The hens, however, are furious. By mid morning, a milky sun emerged and a speckling of blue appears in the sky. Feeling my spirits lift with the increasing light levels, I take a walk around the garden after lunch to take stock. A bumblebee queen bustles past me, the first I have seen this year. I was standing next to a tiny patch of celandine, which she investigated before settling on some willow catkins, bursting with pollen. I realise that my garden would benefit from more early flowering plants, for the benefit of the bumblebees as well as for my own mental well-being. I make a note in my diary to look at purchasing some Pulmonaria plants, otherwise known as lungwort, to supply some nectar-laden treats for the insects and some cheerful colour for me. I dig up some raspberry canes from my unruly patch and wrap them in a carrier bag to send to friends who have just moved house, as a garden-warming gift. As I write their new address on the package, it occurs to me that the parcel looks as though it contains a severed limb and I hope their postman has a suitably dark sense of humour.

March is the month when my gardening year really begins to take off. I make a start by cutting back in the borders now that the bulbs and new growth are beginning to appear through the soil. It is also a good time, on the more clement days, to do a spot of weeding, or plant editing as I prefer to think of it. I allow some weeds to reside in my borders and tend only to remove those I find to be problematic, such as couch grass, nettles, thistles and dock. This leaves plenty of scope to leave a few native plants in amongst those you have planted. My favourites for leaving in the borders are herb Robert, red campion, dead nettles, both white- and red-flowered and cow parsley. I once heard someone say that if you want to get rid of all the weeds in your garden, then you should simply refer to them as wild flowers. While I could never have managed to get away with leaving weeds in the flower borders of many of the gardens I have worked in, the fact that I can do this in my own garden feels bold and adventurous. I like being mindfully neglectful; I embrace the wild edges and revel in the chaotic disorder of a more natural display. The bumblebee clearly agrees, as she reappears again on the surprisingly pretty flowers of red dead nettle, her long tongue probing the inner regions of the bloom. I smile and greet her as 'Your Majesty' as she flies off to her underground burrow, pollen sacs laden, in readiness for her egg-laying spree. Those weeds I have declined to keep in situ are dumped unceremoniously into a bucket of water to drown them. This serves two purposes, firstly to kill off the weeds, some of which can be rather too resilient for my liking and can regrow even after several months in the compost heap. A drowned weed never returns and after a week or two of being submerged, the resulting slightly stinky brew can be safely put on the compost heap as an excellent compost activator, full of beneficial organisms and nutrients.

Cutting back

This is one of those jobs which, when I was a professional gardener, used to be done at the end of the growing year in autumn. I now prefer to leave this until early spring. Tidiness is not something we should be aiming for in our gardens and leaving plants to die back is an essential component of natural gardening. Can you learn to appreciate the form of dead flower heads, skeletal stems and the slow collapse of the border's previously voluptuous structure? Leaving all of this in situ until the last minute before everything begins to grow again enables us to seek the beauty in the death and decay part of the big cycle of life and seasons. It is also, as we know, good for invertebrate life and the soil. I specifically plant perennials which leave architectural forms through the winter time, my favourites being the old flower heads of *Rudbeckias*, *Eryngiums* and Jerusalem sage or *Phlomis*, especially in midwinter when they are bejewelled with frost or snow. I have also noticed that the goldfinches seem to love these old flower stems too, as they take their time slowing picking seeds out of the old inflorescences.

Rather than cutting everything and then having to cart it all off to the compost heap, these days I use a technique known as 'chop and drop'. This allows me to conserve my precious energy levels for more important gardening tasks, such as food growing. I'll expand on this further in the section on composting. Sometimes, I allow the old stems of perennial plants to remain as stubby structure, as they act as supports for new growth, preventing them from flopping over later in the year. *Rudbeckia*, *Helenium* and Asters or Michaelmas daisies respond well to this treatment and this technique saves me from needing to put in canes or pea sticks as support later in the season. (Incidentally, asters have now been renamed by botanists as *Symphiotrichum*. I still refer to them as asters because I am an old-fashioned sort of lass.) I then do any necessary weeding in the more formal beds and borders at this point in the season, at a time when they are easy to get to and when the bulbs are sufficiently visible to prevent me trampling them. Being able to identify weeds in their early stages is a useful skill to have, one I have perfected over the years, enabling me to allow self-seeding plants such as poppy, columbine, honesty and foxglove to remain while I evict the unwanted bed fellows before they get too big for their boots.

Weeds

At this point, we should talk about weeds in more detail. The word 'weed' makes me feel a bit sad and confused, as some of my favourite wild flowers are considered weeds by others. As a child, daisies in the lawn were my absolute favourites and red campion is one of my most used plants today. The old saying that a weed is just a plant in the wrong place, doesn't sit comfortably with me either. These native and wild-growing plants have been part of our lives and our landscape for as long as people have been around and many of them were once cultivated or collected for long-forgotten uses in the home.

We need to learn which types of plants will thrive in a low input situation and which wild flowers and 'weeds', if left to grow, will be both beneficial for nature and a source of beauty, without overwhelming the individual plants we have introduced. It can be a fine line that we learn to tread. The more biodiverse plant communities are those which have achieved a level of maturity and stability. Many of our gardens are immature ecosystems, tending to rely on a few pioneer plants, such as nettles, which often out-compete plants which we consider more desirable. These things are part of the fun of learning about how to manage your garden and shouldn't be seen as obstacles to success or rules to abide by.

I invite you to learn about the plants in your space, whether these are intentionally planted, or wild things which have volunteered themselves. While it is useful to know the cultivated plants in the garden, it is far more important to make acquaintance with your wild weeds. Weed is of course a derogatory term which denotes a plant which is allegedly in the wrong place. On the contrary, I suggest that most weeds are exactly where they should be. As wild things which have arrived under their own volition, I suggest that they know better than any of us what they require to grow well, and therefore are quite likely to be in exactly the correct place for themselves. It is the wildings which most frequently bring me pleasure in the garden. Those feral plants which are able to survive the neglect, find their niches and thrive without any input.

Eat your weeds?

Weeds can tell you a lot about the state of your soil and the microclimate in your garden. For instance, nettles are usually a sign of high fertility, while docks and dandelions signify that your ground is compacted and possibly depleted. Those deep tap roots on these plants are intended to break through hard soil and bring nutrients, especially minerals, up from deep in the soil up to the surface. Soil which is regularly disturbed by digging or hoeing is usually a home to a range of annual weeds such as chickweed or groundsel, which are able to grow quickly, cover the ground and flower and set seed within a short time frame. I encourage chickweed in my vegetable plot, as it is a wonderful ground cover and an excellent supplementary feed for hens.

Once you learn what the common wild plants are in your garden, it can suggest to you what types of plants might like to grow there instead of the wild things, or even if there might be some 'weeds' which you are happy to tolerate for either their flowers or else their ability to cover the soil surface and help to regulate the fertility. For example, if you have a fertile area where nettles have been thriving, perhaps this could be a good place to grow vegetables, or annual flowers which prefer rich soils, such as sweet peas or *Dahlia*. I would also hope that if you had the space, that you might be persuaded to leave a few nettles somewhere, particularly as they not only provide food for the caterpillars of many of our butterfly species, but also provide a particularly nutritious food source for humans. I really enjoy eating nettle greens lightly steamed in early spring and use them in soups, curries and pasta dishes where you might normally use spinach. The unripe seeds are edible too; I collect them and dry them, using them as nutty-flavoured sprinkles on breakfast cereal or on top of bread and pies. They are full of goodness and some say that they give a boost to our metabolism, giving us more vital energy. This is precisely the sort of food that I feel my body needs these days and I love the fact that it comes for free, rather than via some over-priced supplement from the health food shop.

The deeply rooted weeds, such as dandelion, are frequently found in grassland which takes a lot of foot traffic. If you have them in your lawn, I usually leave them as they are doing a good job at improving drainage and relieving compaction. Their flowers are cheerful and provide an essential supply of early nectar for emerging bumblebee queens and other species of solitary pollinators in the spring. If you are worried about them seeding everywhere, then the heads can be mown off, if absolutely necessary, once flowering has finished, although again their seed offers a great snack for seed-eating species such as goldfinches. Watching a flock of goldfinches flitting around a meadow, delicately extracting dandelion seed, is a highlight. The collective term for goldfinches is a charm, a most delightful and apt description, as their bright gaudy faces and excitable chattering make for a heart-lifting moment in any ordinary day. I often think that if dandelions were tricky to grow, our Instagram feed would be full of them, as we strive to grow the biggest and best. Unfortunately for dandelions, they are all too easy to grow and therefore we don't treat them with the same reverence we have towards the horticultural divas such as *Dahlias* and *Delphiniums*. In the beds and borders, you can replace them with other deep-rooted plants which will do the same job, such as any of the umbellifers – fennel or sea holly (*Eryngium*) for instance, or *Acanthus*, also known as bear's breeches, a striking evergreen architectural plant with curious purplish flowers in summer. *Inula* (elecampane or elfdock), a bright-yellow statuesque daisy, or *Crambe* (sea kale), with its huge leaves and frothy white flowers, are also deep rooted although these take up a lot of space and aren't really suitable for a small garden. *Primula* make good substitutes where space is at a premium – both the native primrose and cowslip are deeply rooting plants, which also tends to make them drought tolerant, a useful trait in these times of increasingly unpredictable weather.

Areas in your garden that attract a lot of annual weeds can easily be dealt with by substituting the annual weeds that you don't like for annual flowers that you do. The list for these is endless, but if you have a patch of soil which has been bare for some time, then spring or autumn sowing of seed is likely the easiest way to cover the soil and have something nice to look forward to. There are plenty of annual flowers, such as poppies and marigolds, which if left alone will self-seed, saving you the work of re-sowing every year as well as the financial outlay. I hope you now realise that nature tends to avoid bare soil whenever possible. This simply reiterates the fact that fertility is governed by and dependent upon plants and their roots interacting with soil organisms. In order to maintain the best diversity of organisms and therefore fertility for plant life, it is so important that soils are generally covered, if not by plant growth then with some sort of mulch, which in nature is usually leaves.

Where there is a requirement for soil to be kept bare, then we need to use other techniques to offset the depletion which can happen if soil is left open to the elements, especially if it has been disturbed in some way. Mulching will help; materials as diverse as manure, home-made compost, woodchip, straw and cardboard are all suitable mulches – the list is long and doesn't necessarily require money to be spent. The use of green manures, which are plants which are grown as cover, some of which add nutrients to the soil and help to increase organic matter are useful. My own favourites are clover, buckwheat and winter tares. In the vegetable plot, I have a tendency to leave annual weeds until they are large enough to identify and easy to pull up where they're not wanted. This allows soil to retain structure and fertility, encourages soil organisms to stay around and thrive, while the input from the gardener is pretty minimal. I do consider that annual weeds provide a good deal of shelter for young vegetable seedlings, protecting them from the vagaries of the weather, helping draw their growth upwards and confusing any insect pests who are on the lookout for something to munch on. They can be carefully removed if they begin to swamp out those more intentional plantings, but please don't feel that a weedy vegetable plot is something to be ashamed of; the vision of a perfect veggie plot, with neat rows and bare soil between them is an outdated distraction not to mention a waste of time and energy. In reality, I find that a weedy vegetable plot is pretty much as productive as a tidy one and let's face it, a lot less work!

Invitations to celebrate the season

- While it is still early in the year, you should now be able to find signs of imminent growth. One of the first signs of change are the catkins on hazel bushes in the hedgerows. Slowly but surely, they will start to turn yellow with pollen as the season progresses. See if you can find the tiny red tufts of a female hazel flower on the branches once the male catkins are at their peak.

- If you are a grower of vegetables, and you are lucky enough to have a heated propagator or a suitably sunny and warm windowsill, you can consider starting off a few seeds. Chillies, peppers, aubergines and tomatoes can all be started after Imbolc as they are slow growing when young and benefit from an early start. If you have a greenhouse, you can also start off broad beans and early peas in modules for planting out later. Seeing nascent plant life emerging from seed is a gloriously uplifting experience.

- This is a great time to take hard wood cuttings, just before the sap begins to rise. Lots of things can be grown from hardwood cuttings at this time of year, fruiting or flowering currants, *Hydrangea*s, most flowering shrubs, apart from evergreen types, and a wide range of berries. Simply cut stems of last year's growth, just below a bud, allowing around 10–15 centimetres of growth. Insert them either straight into the ground, or into a pot of garden soil, ensuring a third of the length of each cutting is below soil level. Keep them well-watered and by midsummer, they should be in leaf and producing their own roots. Lift them next autumn and plant out in their final place, or pot up to give away to friends and neighbours.

- Early spring flowers lift the spirits after a long winter. Keep an eye out for what flowers early in your community. *Crocus*, snowdrops, *Hellebore* and dwarf iris are all very easy to grow, either in the garden or in pots by the back door. If you don't have enough colour in the garden at this time of year, make a mental note to invest in some early flowering bulbs later in the season, to rectify that lack. The cheapest time to buy hellebores, which are surprisingly expensive, is usually when they have finished flowering and garden centres sell them off cheaply as they no longer look attractive. These flowers also provide essential food for early emerging bumblebee queens too, in case you needed another excuse to shop.

- Have a go at making your own plant fertiliser. When you begin to carry out your spring tidy up of beds and borders, collect any weeds you remove and put them in a bucket of rainwater. Deep-rooted weeds such as dandelions, docks or nettles are an excellent source of nutrients and minerals which can be used as a liquid feed for plants. Brew the weeds for several weeks until the resulting sludge is brown and decayed. Use the liquid in small amounts to add to the watering can, a cup full is sufficient for a 2 litre can. This is a smelly process so don't wear your best clothes in case of spillage! This also makes a great compost activator.

CHAPTER SIX

Ostara: The Spring Equinox

This is the quickening of the year, the time when change occurs so rapidly it can leave us breathless as we watch it unfurling before our eyes. The equinox is when the light and dark is held in balance; day and night are of equal length. I am learning that I prefer these days of equity and balance and I relish the gentle rhythms as the seasons turn. In my younger days, it was the solstice celebrations I enjoyed with their extremes; both the white-hot light of midsummer and the wild darkness of Yule were celebrated furiously. Lately, I have begun to feel more at home in the middles rather than the peaks; I appreciate the edges of the change of season and find them to be more beautiful and multi-layered.

March can be a changeable month up here on the moors and I must be careful not to get ahead of myself with planting things out. The sap is most certainly rising though, the birds are busy with beaks full of nesting materials, the gentle hum of bumblebees exploring the garden for nectar-laden treats surrounds me and it is difficult not to be caught up in the frenzy. Finding a gentle balance is essential to be sure that I don't weary too quickly of the garden and the ever-lengthening list of jobs which coincides with the extending daylight hours and warmer temperatures.

The day dawned full of rosy pink promise, and as I rose from my bed, the sun rose too. The epitome of a perfect spring day. Warm enough to work in shirt sleeves, as long as you stayed in the sun and kept out of the still chilly breeze. The soil is dry, there has been little rain this month, despite threatening clouds, and the gusty winds have eclipsed my memories of squelching through ankle deep mud to the polytunnel, which was a daily occurrence last month. It's perfect for a day out in nature and despite the reports I should be writing, I decide to spend a pleasant day at home gardening rather than in front of a computer screen, since I have the flexibility to order my working week to suit myself, something I have learnt to do in order to manage my illness around my business. Feeling the sun on my back and soaking up the sights and sounds of spring becomes my priority because I think life is short and days like this are a gift to be taken full advantage of.

My windowsills are crammed with trays and pots of seedlings. I feel like the botanical shepherdess of my growing flock of tiny plants, ushering them around and tending to their needs. The greenhouse shelving is filling up nicely and I find myself doing a shuttle dance between the house and greenhouse every morning and evening, to put the seedlings out before breakfast, in order that they not become too leggy and etiolated for lack of light on the windowsills and needing to bring them in at night as the temperatures are still far too low for the tender seedlings of tomato, courgette and chilli. In the polytunnel, I have a few hardy salad leaves growing, wild rocket, mizuna and a type of mild mustard called Red Frills. There are also a few edible wild things emerging now, mainly wild garlic and cleavers, which make good eating at this time of year. I pick a small handful for my lunch, rinse them under the tap and eat them with my sandwiches knowing that not only do they taste amazing but they are fresh, nutrient dense and have cost me very little, either in effort or financially. These little things can make such a difference to our health and well-being and I can't recommend more highly that you try this for yourself.

Pricking out seedlings

Probably my least favourite job in the greenhouse, after cleaning the algae-covered glass at the end of summer, the task of selecting the strongest seedlings and transferring them into new pots is a requisite part of growing plants from seed. Faced with several trays of overcrowded seedlings, this can seem like a repetitive and mundane task. To begin with, I don't mind and take great satisfaction in the exercise, but after several hours, even if I'm listening to music or a podcast, I feel my enthusiasm for the task begin to dwindle. Approaching this with care and attention to the potential of each seedling to produce something beautiful, useful, or both can transform this job into something more fundamental to us. Thinking about the parts of these tiny plants, and what their function is, can allow us to explore our own role and surroundings. Think about how we might be better able to flourish in improved conditions. How can we change things to improve our ability to thrive?

The most important part of any tiny seedling is the roots. Without strong roots, we cannot grow. We talk about understanding our own roots, as being linked to our heritage, somewhere we have come from, the place where our ancestors dwelt or the town in which we grew up. Sometimes this link to the past can often be problematic for many reasons and I prefer to consider roots as where we choose to anchor ourselves now, rather than being stuck with an historical account of where we have travelled from. In pricking out, we can learn that it is possible to be moved and regrow roots in a new place and that this might be better for us as individuals, rather than being crowded together with others from the same seed packet! Ensuring that the place where you choose to put down your roots is beneficial and nurturing is essential. Why make it difficult to grow and find stability? It is always worth remembering too that the Latin name for roots is *radix*, which also gave us the word radical, meaning holding a strong belief in effecting and causing change in a progressive way. We can think of it, therefore, as reconnecting with nature by familiarising ourselves with the growing of plants, the following of the seasons and taking responsibility for the stewardship of the earth as a radical pursuit.

As someone who believes that we should be practising gardening by allowing nature to play a leading role, I would be proud to be considered as a radical gardener.

The next thing to consider are the leaves; these are the engine room, the precious source of photosynthesis, the miracle that turns sunlight into energy which plants use to grow. From huge great trees to the vegetables on your plate, without leaves they wouldn't exist. Care is needed to ensure that leaves are undamaged and can provide sufficient energy to the seedling in order to grow well. Ensuring that we create the very best growing conditions is a priority, to avoid transplant shock, that period of adjusting to a new environment, which occurs when we move seedlings or even ourselves to new places in order to encourage better growth. Seedling leaves are tiny and care needs to be taken when handling them, so that they can take full advantage of the opportunity in which to grow larger. Consider the situation they are growing in; adequate light and warmth is essential, away from harmful draughts or fluctuating temperatures. Once growing well, and the first true leaves have appeared, a seedling needs to be hardened off. This is a little like expanding your comfort zone. Staying in ideal growing conditions can make new growth soft and liable to damage. Gradual movement towards more realistic conditions allows a seedling to toughen up slowly, without damage, and develop sufficient strength to deal with a range of conditions which might not be ideal.

Finally, I invite you to consider trying to raise all the seedlings you have grown (unless you have gone overboard on the seeds) or at least vary your reasons for selecting some over others. As gardeners, we are often taught to only spend our efforts on the strongest and most uniform of seedlings, selecting the best then discarding the rest. I challenge you to think differently about this. As we now realise, diversity is the key to making resilient systems in nature. There is a need for a broad spectrum of plants, each with their individual characteristics. Particularly when it comes to growing flowers, some of the most beautiful and unusual blooms have resulted from those seedlings which might have been in the 'discard' pile. Yes, they might have taken a bit longer to catch up to the others, but if I hadn't given them that bit more TLC, then I wouldn't have had the wonderful diversity of colour and form that I enjoy now.

April used to bring rain showers, but in these last few years it has been a cold dry month. The lack of rain and overnight frosts means that very little is growing yet. The tiny flock of hardy Hebridean sheep, which we keep to lightly graze one of our fields, started lambing at the end of March. Today the last ewe, who we call April, because that is when she has her lambs, had twins. When I was asked at school at the age of 4, what I wanted to be when I grew up, I clearly remember confidently replying with 'The Queen'. On being told by my teacher the news that a working-class girl from Doncaster wasn't going to be in with a chance to fulfil that dream, I bit my lip, thought for a while and answered, 'A shepherdess?' The teacher sighed deeply and moved on to the next child. I guess she did me a favour that day by not shattering that dream too.

Today, finally, I became a shepherdess, fifty years on from vocalising that childhood dream. I was sitting eating my lunch, gazing out of the window when I realised that April was missing from the flock. I put down my mug of tea and went out to look. Sure enough, there she was at the far end of the field at the foot of a steep bank in a tangle of thorns, with two wet lambs. The forecast was for sleet and snow showers overnight, so I needed to bring them under cover. I inched slowly down the bank and picked up both lambs, still sticky and damp, and tucked them in my best jumper. I walked them back to the field shelter, their mother furious at my intervention, butting my legs and blocking my way as the twins bleated loudly. Eventually, after having to placate the ram, who as head of the flock thought I was a lamb thief, I managed to get mother and both babies into the shelter, my heart thumping. Food and water were brought for Mum and extra hay bedding for the lambs. As they started to suckle, I realised this was the best feeling in the world, or at least as good as tree planting in the top ten of life-affirming moments, anyway. It's at times like these that I realise that although my choice of lifestyle has not made for an easy life, especially with a chronic illness snapping at my heels, I wouldn't change it for anything.

April is a capricious month on the moors, fluctuating wildly between cold, grey, sleety days, where winter appears to pop back into the fray, saying, 'Wait, I haven't gone yet,' and those heart-filling, mood-boosting, blue sky days where the thrill of the new season fills me with such joy. The thing with spring is that once she arrives, she is like a whirlwind blowing in, she doesn't drag her feet. It feels as though it was winter only a couple of weeks ago and now the land is fizzing with energy, the familiar stark outlines of winter now becoming hazy with a luminescent green veil. Unstoppable now, the big reveal is underway. Each day brings a new vista, a fresh colour scheme, a renewal. The slow flourish picks up pace like bubbles rising in a newly opened bottle of verdant Champagne, over flowing its container and pouring its frothy green contents over the landscape. The leaves emerge in concert and join the symphony in every imaginable shade of green. The garden is like a slow-motion firework and it keeps getting better every day.

Permaculture principle: Use and value renewables and resources

This permaculture principle encourages us to ensure that we are using things which have a cyclical lifespan rather than items which use lots of resources and are not able to be reused in some way. From the electricity we consume to the packaging we buy items in, it asks us to consider the impact these items have and how best we can reuse and recycle. In gardening, there are plenty of options that allow use to be thrifty and resourceful in our use of items. Making our own compost for seed sowing, reusing containers for growing in, cultivating plants such as comfrey in order to make our own liquid fertiliser and saving our own seed are all small but effective ways to become less dependent on needing to buy in things for the garden.

I begin the year by saving the cardboard inners from toilet roll, ready for sowing sweet peas. These are one of the few things I start off early in the year, as they require a long growing period; once they have germinated, they are surprisingly hardy and I can grow them on in my unheated greenhouse. Not long afterwards, I start the onion seed for the same reason. I save the plastic carton from the mushrooms you buy from the supermarket as they have more depth than the average seed tray, which enables me to grow the onion seedlings in that container for longer, before needing to transplant them later in the year – once the soil warms up.

Recently, I have found that shop-bought peat-free compost is becoming very variable in its quality and have become quite angry at times when I have spent time and effort growing things from seed, only to realise that the compost they are in is adversely affecting their growth. I have begun to collect leaves in the autumn and I put them in an old compost sack in order to create my own leaf mould to use for potting compost, which is a splendid way of reusing both leaves and plastic bags, which are often considered waste items, in order to make something useful and valuable. I also collect mole hill soil for the same purpose. I get around the fact that it is frequently full of weed seeds by spreading it out in a seed tray and allowing the weeds to germinate. I then weed the soil before using it in my seed-sowing mix.

Compost corner

Making compost is one of the most requested topics from anyone who is considering becoming more organic and eco-friendlier in the garden. While there are dozens of different types of composting equipment available for gardeners to buy, all of which claim to unlock the secrets of this alchemic process, the truth is simply that composting is a natural process. It is carried out by a wide range of organisms called detritivores or 'rotters' which nature manages perfectly well without any help from manufactured equipment. The issue is typically that we tend to want it to happen in a hurry and not only that, we also expect it to look like the pristine organic matter which we buy in plastic bags at the garden centre. Compost is frequently referred to as 'Black Gold' which is presumably why we are so attracted to making it, being gardening alchemists. Well-made compost is a powerhouse of fertility and contains a multitude of organisms all of which will help to create a healthy soil environment.

Simply put, if any form of carbon-rich material is left in a pile with sufficient water and air for the decomposing organisms to work effectively, then composting is what will take place. The problems begin when we allow the pile to become too wet, too dry or else we use too much of a nitrogen-rich material, such as grass clippings alone. It is then that we end up with undecomposed matter or a stinky slimy mess which isn't really what we had in mind. Instead of the *Great British Bake Off* which has enthralled so many people on television, I suggest that maybe it is time for the great British Compost Challenge. This could potentially encourage more of us to take part in this ultimate recycling event and strip away a lot of the myths and misunderstandings surrounding it.

The very best and simplest forms of compost making are uncomplicated piles of mixed vegetation. Preferably there will be a mix of what gardeners tend to refer to as 'Greens and Browns'. Greens are fresh living leaves and vegetation of all types, including vegetable waste. As they are rich in nitrogen, these are mainly decomposed by bacteria, which require some moisture and air in order to start their work. Frequently, this type of material heats up when wet and then becomes compacted, excluding air from the heap. Mixing in carbon-rich material such as wood chip, torn up paper or cardboard, dead leaves and stems enables the heap to remain quite open and airy. It also encourages fungal organisms to join in the decomposition process. Ideally, the best way to make an effective compost pile is to collect all the material together in one go and layer it up to make a large and well-mixed heap. Make sure it's thoroughly damp throughout, cover it with carpet or an old plastic compost sack weighed down and wait.

Rocket fuel

There are ways of speeding up and encouraging your compost pile to become more efficient. One of the best kick starters for a sluggish compost pile is urine. This is, naturally, a free resource available to everyone, full of nitrogen and beneficial to encouraging bacterial action in the heap. Can you encourage the men folk in your life to use the compost pile as a urinal, or will this upset the neighbours? I have a memory of telling one of my neighbours about this and one evening, while sitting quietly, I heard a knock on the window. My neighbour was leaning over the fence, waving a jug of steaming yellow liquid at me. With a big smile and a thumbs-up, he toddled off down the garden to pour it on the compost pile. He made great compost that year and his vegetables were abundant and healthy. If this makes you feel squeamish, then there are various products available to buy in garden centres, which although require you to spend cash, they will fulfil the same requirement, although I am only aware of one which is urine based.

Compost usually takes between six and twelve months to be ready. There are, of course, special insulated bins which claim to create compost in less time than that, but in my experience, this is unusual. Unless you are planning to make your own potting compost, it doesn't actually matter if it isn't completely 'finished'. A slightly chunkier and less rotted compost is just as good for your soil, and therefore your plants, as anything which is a fine, brown, crumbly texture, which is the nirvana of composting. A rougher mix acts perfectly well as a mulch on top of soil and despite suggestions to the contrary, I don't believe that it encourages more slugs or woodlice which will then rampage through your seedlings, as this has most definitely not been the case in my experience.

Adding food waste to the compost is usually not advised as this is likely to attract rats to your compost area. Most people do, and indeed should, add vegetable peelings and such like, as it adds a good amount of nutrients to the mix and is something which definitely doesn't need carting off by the council to go into landfill sites. To avoid the addition of food waste being a problem, there are various ways of ensuring this isn't an issue, using either Bokashi bins to compost this or else a wormery or hot composter. All of these basically speed up the process, are made in sealed bins which are rodent-proof and are efficient ways of dealing with organic waste from the kitchen.

The use of Bokashi or 'effective microorganisms', known as EM for short, is a method of composting which pre-ferments vegetable waste before it is added to the compost bin or placed directly in or on the soil. This is an anaerobic fermentation using selected microorganisms, so is usually carried out in a sealed bin to prevent too much air getting to it. The EM usually come as a bran which has been pre-inoculated, which is then added to the kitchen waste in layers, although you can also buy it as a liquid spray. Once it has fermented for around two weeks, it starts to smell a bit pickle like or vinegary and is often covered by a fuzzy white mould, although the contents themselves will look pretty much the same as when you put them in. However, once exposed to the air the contents will break down very quickly and are an excellent way to jump start your compost pile. They are also very effective in the bottom of holes for tree or shrub planting, or shallow trenches for growing beans and peas, although this would probably be frowned upon by evangelical no-diggers!

A hot bin is essentially a very well-insulated composting vessel. It comes complete with a kick-starting liquid, which presumably is a mix of suitable microorganisms and a bulking agent, which is woodchip. It enables the composting of both cooked and raw food safely and claims to produce compost in 30–90 days. As with all composting endeavours, mixing together the right combination of ingredients appears to be the key to success. The benefit of hot composting is that you can monitor the temperature within the bin and it generally runs hot enough to kill off any weed seeds in garden waste.

Wormeries are yet another composting route available to the home gardener. These are generally enclosed bins, sometimes with trays stacked on top of each other, where vegetable waste is added in layers for composting worms to break down. Wormeries are a good option for those with tiny gardens, especially if you are a container grower, as they produce a very nutrient-rich compost, perfect for topping-up pots and raised beds. Many commercially available wormeries have taps which enable you to draw off liquid formed as part of the process, which can be used as a liquid feed. The downsides to wormeries is that the process is fairly slow and doesn't produce a great deal of compost, although it is of fantastic quality. Composting worms are also quite fussy about their diet and will not tolerate citrus fruit in any form or anything from the onion family as it is far too acidic for them and probably gives them crippling indigestion. They are, however, quite happy if their food has been fermented with Bokashi first and this has the added advantage of speeding up the time it takes for the worms to break down the vegetable matter. Wormeries obviously contain live creatures and do require some looking after.

They prefer stable temperatures, so may need to be kept under cover through the winter months and they don't like too much rain either. Fair weather composters they may be, but they are a useful tool in the organic gardener's kit.

Another route to composting or perhaps even bypassing the composting method, especially in established borders, is to do something called 'chop and drop'. As mentioned earlier it's something I do a lot in my own garden as it takes significantly less effort. This is simply a method of cutting back herbaceous growth at the end of winter and simply laying it on top of the soil around the plants that it came from. This acts like a mulch and soon rots down to feed the soil. It is, in fact, nature's own recycling in action, where the nutrients are taken up and deposited by plants in a seasonal cycle. Bacteria and fungi absorb the nutrients from the decaying matter and are in turn consumed by other organisms, leading to the nutrients being deposited again for plants to take advantage of during the active growing season. I find that spring bulbs are quite happy to grow up through it without any problem and if it is done late enough in the year, it is fairly well decomposed already and doesn't blow around in windy days. A scythe or hedge trimmer are quite good tools for this job as it means you can cut back quite quickly without needing to stand on the borders. It saves a lot of time and energy as the gardener doesn't have to collect the clippings and move them to a compost bin, then wait a few months before transporting the compost back to where it was in the first place.

Tea, Vicar?

Compost teas are something else you might have heard about. These, despite the name, are not something nourishing for the gardener to sup on in between work but are intended to boost the population of effective organisms in the soil. They are created by mixing completed compost with water and preferably bubbling air through it by means of an aerator, similar to the set-up you would find in a fish tank. They are frequently used by regenerative growers, especially in the early days of transitioning away from chemical-based growing, as a means of improving biologically depleted soils. There are also various products which you can buy which have a similar effect when either added to your own compost bins, or added to soils and other growing media. Some of these come as biologically active, concentrated composts or teas to be watered down and added directly to soils where they are required. There is a strand of regenerative growing called Korean Natural Farming which is based on the use of soil amendments, built on what are known as indigenous microorganisms, which are essentially cultures taken from locally occurring healthy soils. Some people, when making their compost teas, add a small amount of soil from an area which hasn't seen much in the way of chemical additives, such as ancient woodland. This is seen as a way of increasing and encouraging microorganisms that are adapted and naturally suited to the local environment as a way of improving soil and plant health. The fundamental aim of Korean Natural Farming is to boost the biological functions of plant- and soil health so that plants and crops are healthier, pathogens are kept at bay and chemical interventions are no longer needed or even seen as desirable. Again, this is a topic which is vast in its scope and I heartily recommend that if your interest has been piqued by this brief discussion, then there are plenty of more in-depth books and online articles, which can answer most of your questions.

Permaculture principle: Design from patterns to details

This principle asks us to always look at the bigger picture when designing something new, rather than getting bogged down in the details. Standing back and looking at the whole can allow us to be much more holistic in our thinking. Nature is great at producing patterns, many of which repeat themselves in the most unlikely ways. Consider the way that veins in a leaf are laid out, when we hold them up to the light. Then contrast this pattern with the way a river becomes an estuary when it meets the sea, or the way that our own veins are laid out for the transport of blood around our body. Another favourite of mine are the frost ferns which form on my car windscreen in frosty weather. Their intricate forms resemble the fronds of ferns so closely that it is a wonderful reminder that growth proliferates from simple structures if allowed to and that change can bring great abundance and a beautiful complexity. These patterns all have close similarities in both their form and function. See if you can see any patterns in the way that nature creates growing spaces and see if there might be something you can copy in your own garden.

One of the most common patterns in life is that of the spiral, especially in the design of snail shells. A spiral can echo the cyclical nature of the seasons as well as our own learning curves while we learn to garden with nature as our teacher. While we might feel that travelling in circles gets you nowhere, a spiral can show you that although you might have come around to what appears like the same place, you are in fact experiencing it differently as time has passed and you have become wiser and more knowledgeable.

Permaculture also uses spirals to teach us about microclimate. Herb spirals are a common way of being able to grow a variety of plants with differing requirements in one place. The spiral is based on a mound of soil, which casts shade, allowing for more moisture-loving plants to thrive in these areas, whereas the top and sunnier sides offer the correct conditions for those plants which require full sun and better drainage.

This principle also reminds me that it is a good thing to stop and zoom out from time to time to take a look at the broader perspective. In the garden, as well as in life, we so easily fall into the trap of just seeing what is in front of our noses and while close observation is useful, sometimes the situation asks us to stand up, walk around a little and view whatever it is that is troubling us from a different perspective. This is a useful principle when planning your garden and one which I didn't take enough notice of when I first arrived here on the land. I rushed into planting far too many things, knowing that I had a big blank canvas to fill. I created borders and crammed them with plants and it was only much later after my diagnosis, when I was at my lowest ebb, that I realised that I had taken on far too much and that I wasn't going to be able to maintain it. At the time, this felt to me like a huge failure and I started to listen to people who told me that what I wanted to do with the garden was too ambitious. 'Keep it small,' they said, 'limit yourself.' I was utterly depressed by this prospect and it took a lot of soul searching for me to see a way through this tangle of what I wanted and what I was capable of at the time. Eventually, it was my rebellious inner teenager which stuck two fingers up to the naysayers and I continued to plant things regardless of the critics, although this time I did have an intuitive sense to take a longer view of what I wanted to achieve. It was then that I decided that my garden would be the biggest experiment in my long and varied horticultural life and that perhaps it would help me to finally bring together the two sides of my deep-seated love for wild nature and my enduring obsession with plants and growing. Looking back this was all the motivation I needed to change my view that my illness was the only narrative in my life and this gave me the enthusiasm to keep trying, learning alternative approaches and inventing a happier ending to the story.

Be wilder

The French have a wonderful word for messy and unkempt which I now use to describe my style of gardening. It is *Bordelique* which to my ears sounds much more romantic and adventurous than untidy. A more bordelique approach to the garden is likely to attract an abundance of nature in the form of insects and birds. It is less likely to need pesticides and fertilisers as nature is able to adapt to a wide range of situations much more successfully than we can with our chemical 'fixes'. It is able to function in harmony with nature where left to its own devices more frequently, it is rare that pests and diseases get out of hand and require the intervention of humans. The word *bordello*, meaning a house of ill repute, also stems from the same root. I love the allusion of sexy fun and joyousness in this and perhaps a bordello in our borders is precisely what nature needs to get back on track!

I suggest that it is perhaps only your neighbours and allotment committee who are likely to cause you problems in taking a more natural approach to gardening. Adopting an alternative angle to managing land always invites comment and potentially criticism from people who have become used to the way things were done in the past. Being mindful in the garden is, I think, the best way to deal with human misunderstandings, allowing you the headspace to be less reactive to complaints, so you can respond with tact, humility and patience. You will be able to explain to your neighbours the reasons behind your seeming neglect and the absolute urgency of creating a diverse habitat for nature wherever we are able to and that this not only benefits wildlife but our own health and well-being too. Be bold and courageous, remain curious, and remember that the alchemists of old were highly misunderstood too.

It's late April. Clearly spring was getting a bit big for her boots, in too much of a rush, the warm sunshine chivvying along the buds to open a little too soon. Nature decides to call a quick break, to slow things down a little, catch her breath. Now the winds swing between the north and the east, turning down the temperature a notch or two. The blossom is superb this year. The Magnolia stellata has been in blossom for weeks with barely a touch of frost damage on the ivory white petals to spoil their perfection. Sargent's cherry (Prunus sargentii) has been and gone already, the shell-pink petals blowing in the wind like confetti, the bronze leaves unfurling in their wake. The Amelanchiers are earning their keep with constellations of tiny white stars, catching the light against the blue of the sky. The pear and damson blossom has already gone over and I cross my fingers for fruit this year. It is the turn now for the bird cherry (Prunus padus) to bloom, a lovely native tree, known locally as wild lilac. I have planted the species as well as a its sporty cousin, 'Colorata', pink in flower with rusty-coloured leaves. It is four years since I began planting them all, as tiny shrubs and trees into the long grass, with only a picture in my head of how it might look. A leap of faith was how it felt at the time and now they are beginning to poke their heads above the parapet of vegetation, making their presence felt and confirming my faith in nature's ability to thrive despite the conditions they encountered.

It's often at times like these, when spring is on surge mode and when everything seems to be growing on steroids and I feel powerless to keep on top of things that I question the choices I have made. Gardening connects us with nature and improves our well-being, but is it worth the time and effort and, perhaps more challenging, why do I bother? This question returns to me whenever I find myself wondering why I grow a bit of lettuce or a few sweet peas when I can just as easily buy a bunch of flowers or a mixed salad bag from the supermarket. Somehow, the value of growing these things for ourselves provides so much more than just the produce we receive as the harvest. I certainly know that I prefer to channel my efforts into growing a few vegetables to supplement my diet than having to spend time queuing in a supermarket chain where the produce has been sitting in plastic bags on a shelf. There is pure joy to be found in the process of growing plants and spending time in the garden, even if the tasks are quite mundane. One of these options is, I believe, much more life enhancing than the other. Can I encourage you to try both and see which works for you?

Whenever I pick up my trowel or allow a flower to remain after its prime, so I can collect seed for the following year, I am transported in my mind to those generations of gardeners and growers who went before me. There is something in all of us connecting us to our ancestors and how they lived upon the land and I feel that I am following in their footsteps. Nature moves to a different cadence, a rhythm as old as life itself, ancient cycles of growth, senescence, death and renewal, always coming full circle with nothing to divide beginnings from endings. We are part of nature and these cycles affect us, no matter how we try to deny them. Dancing with the seasons, each with its own beat, we are more able to feel connected. Driven by the slow twirl between the sun and the earth, we celebrate each season in its turn, from spring into summer, the heady hum of growth and fecundity. Autumn brings fire, the foliar flames flickering and bright, before winter's descent into the dark and dormant days. Acknowledging and celebrating these moments while spending time in nature brings us a sense of calm and comfort, even within the uncertainty and sense of loss that we are currently experiencing in our rapidly changing world.

Is there anything more life affirming than planting seeds and watching them grow, or seeing a bird sitting in a tree which you yourself have planted? Celebrate these small things because they are so important in bringing a sense of accomplishment and nature connection in our daily lives. Nature should make us enchanted. Its beauty and delicate detail, its subtle changes and spontaneity can cast a magic spell over us, enticing us to stay, watch and play. It empowers us and teaches us that we can and do make a difference, and that all the small things we do add up.

Invitations to celebrate the season

- Nettles and wild garlic. This is the season to forage for wild spring greens. Wild garlic – or ramsons – is one of the easiest wild plants to identify and is frequently found in woodland and hedgerows; its pale green leaves have an unmistakable aroma of garlic which becomes stronger as the plant comes into flower. I love to use it in all sorts of dishes, from scrambled eggs to pesto. I also love to pick the first shoots of nettles, which I use instead of spinach in a wide range of dishes. You'll need to wear gloves to pick it, but once boiled in water, it loses its sting. It's a great source of vitamins and minerals, just right to give you a healthy boost after a winter of starchy vegetables. Check carefully that you have identified it correctly and wash well before using.

- Sow more seeds. From flowers to vegetables and herbs, the seed-sowing season is now officially open for business.

- Make the most of warm sunny days and begin to tidy up your beds and borders, ready for the start of the growing season. Use the chop and drop method if you are cutting back old stems, or else make sure you compost as much as you can.

- It's not too late to lift and divide any herbaceous plants which are getting too large and are outgrowing their allotted space. Replant somewhere else, or give the spares away to friends and neighbours to add some diversity for their own gardens.

- Plant any old potatoes that have begun to sprout, into large pots. These will give you some delicious baby new potatoes in around ten weeks' time. Free food always tastes better.

- Find a tree in blossom and sit beneath it. Listen to the bees delighting in its blooms and admire the sun as it shines through the delicate petals.

BELTANE

CHAPTER SEVEN

Beltane

Falling midway between the spring equinox and the summer solstice, this ancient fire festival of 1ˢᵗ May is still celebrated in many parts of the country by dancing, lighting bonfires and gathering around a maypole. This festival celebrated fertility and was deemed to the time when Brigid, the goddess of summer, took the throne, banishing the old crone of winter, and heralding the coming months of growth, abundance and light.

I rise before the dawn and walk up the hill from the cottage, looking down the softly rolling valley towards the sea, to watch the sun rise and welcome in the May. The light wind is coming in from the north-east, making it feel cool despite the bright sun, but the day bodes well and my spirits are high. As I walk back down the track towards home for a cup of tea, I am delighted to see a pair of newly returned swallows chattering excitedly on the overhead wires. I speak welcoming words to them and wish them a successful brood as they fly into the sheep field to check if last year's old nest in the shelter is still suitable.

The apple blossom is starting to burst out of its tight buds and I cross my fingers that the temperatures warm up sufficiently for the bees to find and pollinate the trees. I planted the orchard in a place where I thought it would look good, although until the hedge gets established the trees stand in one of the windiest parts of the garden. Rushing into planting in a new garden, almost always leads to regret, but in this instance, I am unlikely to rectify the situation by moving the trees, so I will have to be patient and wait for the dynamic and microclimate to change as the plants grow. One of the first apple trees I planted up there, a Newton Wonder, already has grown into a dramatic windswept shape, reminding me of the twisted and tortured hawthorns on the Atlantic edge of Penwith in Cornwall, where I used to live. No wonder, then, that the bees are reluctant to venture up there apart from on the most beautiful and still days. One day I will be gathering buckets full of apples from them, but for now I will simply admire their floral display.

May steps into my life like a new lover, provoking an almost feverish joy. Rain showered with gentle kisses and arm wrapped in sun-warmed ecstatic embraces. Each bud is offered as a gift, unwrapped slowly to reveal the treasures held within. The few tulips which the badgers haven't devoured are making a small but colourful show in the border by the stream. They are flamboyant presences with gaudy and generous petals. Presenting themselves slowly, they transition from demure buds, tightly wrapped with streamlined poise to inappropriately lavish blooms, lolling and splayed like frilly pants beneath petticoats. I shiver with delight at the experience, but the ones I planted in pots to keep the scavenging wildlife at bay still have a long way to go yet.

I hear the first cuckoo in the distance, somewhere across the valley; a sound which marks the cusp of summer better than any other. As I check my social media, I am heartened to see a slew of hashtags encouraging no-mow May, asking us to keep the mower in the shed, and highlighting the beauty of a more natural patch of grass and flowers instead of the uniform dull stripes of a static monoculture lawn.

I swear every year that May is my favourite month, although in reality I love them all. Each year I find myself marvelling at the range of green displayed by the freshly clad trees and shrubs. Green is such an under-rated colour in the garden, yet spring green in all its various hues always makes me stop and admire the light which seems to come from within it. White is the perfect accompaniment to all this verdancy – the froth of cow parsley in the hedges and verges, the frills of hawthorn blossom, from a distance looking like drifting snow at the edges of the fields.

Lawns versus meadows

No-mow May has gained in popularity among my gardening community recently and I like to think of it as a gentle invitation to make the transition towards a time when the majority of people finally make the decision that keeping on top of a lawn is not worth the effort. I would like to make a controversial statement here, but I think that lawns are a massive waste of time and energy and not worth the hours spent on mowing, feeding, weeding and edging. Please don't misunderstand me, I think that a nicely clipped lawn is a beautiful thing, it creates a fabulous backdrop to colourful herbaceous borders and in some instances has the effect of accentuating any changes in level within the garden, which wouldn't be so noticeable otherwise. Do we all need to have this as a main feature in the garden though? I suggest not, particularly when people tell me that they want a low-maintenance garden and that they would like more colour. The number of gardens in suburbia which only consist of lawn and fencing or hedges is pitifully high. As a country, I do wonder why we are so hung up on having lawns, particularly perfect ones. We spend in excess of £500 per person per year in the UK on our gardens, the majority of this on lawn care, whether we do this ourselves or employ a firm to do it for us. In the United States, where lawns are an even bigger feature, they spend more on lawn care as a country than they do on foreign aid and it is estimated that an acre of lawn is more expensive to maintain than an acre of corn, rice or sugarcane is to produce. Why on earth, in these days of planetary concern and climate change, are we still so obsessed with growing manicured grass as an ornamental feature?

Lawns became fashionable during the eighteenth century when large landowners started developing landscape gardens which had a naturalistic feel to them. While grasslands on such estates used to be simply grazed short by sheep or cattle in the wider landscape, when the large manor houses and castles were being built for their wealthy owners, these people didn't want to have animals close to their houses, with the noise, smell and mess that comes with them as part of the package. It was then that these wealthy landowners used cheap labour to scythe the grass short in the gardens around their dwellings, giving the same effect as grazing animals, without any of the unpleasant drawbacks. Obviously, this was a costly venture and only the most well-heeled could pay the wages of a team of men with scythes. In time, of course, this became mechanised and the invention of mowing machinery began to make this landscape feature more accessible. Fast forward a couple of centuries and we find ourselves in the situation where almost everyone with a garden has a lawn, almost as a default position. We find vast numbers of lawns in public spaces and increasingly we find road verges treated as lawns too, clipped short to 'keep them tidy'.

Dandelions

Try taking a different road out of town and drive into the countryside rather than the garden centre and see if you can find some inspiration in a patch of wildness somewhere that you admire. Even a roadside verge can be inspiring sometimes. Verges are a wonderful local habitat, if left unmown, and they act as corridors for wildlife to traverse through. One day I was driving down a busy dual carriage way with my mum sitting next to me in the car. It was one of those brilliantly bright days at the start of spring and it felt good to be out and about. She had been diagnosed with Alzheimer's disease a few years earlier and this enabled her to perceive things in different ways to other people. Dementia can remove social filters, often leading to unusual behaviour patterns and thoughts. As we drove along, singing along to songs on the radio, she suddenly noticed a broad swathe of bright-yellow flowers growing in the grass alongside the road. Captivated by this joyful sight, she wondered out loud as to who had spent so much time planting all these wonderful flowers and commented on what a great idea it was for cheering up the roadside verges. It was a sunny day and the flowers in question were dandelions in full bloom. It was an inspired piece of planting, the golden braid of flowers fringing the edges reminded me of the gold leaf on the rim of my mother's favourite teacup and saucer. My mother didn't believe me that they were weeds or even wild flowers, so I didn't argue. After all, she was correct in her view that they were a thing of great beauty. I think that sometimes we label and categorise things in a derogatory way which prevents us from being able to see their true elegance and style.

Love your lawn?

A good old-fashioned lawn, unimproved by fertiliser or weed killer, containing a plethora of diminutive wild flowers such as patches of daisies, the purple domes of selfheal, a scattering of sky-blue speedwells and golden hop trefoil is, however, a different situation. Rare though these environments now are, they do still exist in some older gardens and are an excellent habitat for insects of all types as well as ground-feeding birds such as starlings – with their joyful swagger and beautiful 'oil on water' plumage. So, therefore, if you really do feel that you need to have a lawn, then it would be wonderful if these were the short-cropped diverse swards which offer a home and a food source to so many creatures, rather than the emerald green, weed and moss free toxic monocultures which really don't offer anything to anyone. Plus, let's not even mention plastic grass and astroturf, hey? (Sighs deeply) Lawns do have their place in a garden and I'm not necessarily going to encourage everyone to dump their short grass, but please ask yourself if spending an hour, or more every week through the summer months behind a mower really is the best and most enjoyable use of your precious time.

I remember an occasion when I was working as a head gardener at a National Trust property, where I was in the process of developing wild flower meadows in the orchard. It was midsummer and the peak flowering period had just passed. I was stopped by an elderly visitor, who queried if I was the head gardener. I replied that I was and he nodded at me sighing, before asking me if my mower had broken down and did I need help in fixing it. He went on to berate the mess, as he described it, and told me in no uncertain terms how unkempt and scruffy the garden looked and how I would need to start from scratch with the lawns if I ever wanted to get them back into order. I tried hard to explain what I was doing, but he simply said, meadows are where they graze cows, there is no place for them in a garden. Luckily, ideas have begun to change and the wildflower meadows in this public garden are a well-loved feature, at least by most visitors, and are a refuge and inspiration for people and wildlife alike.

Now that wildflower meadows are becoming a fashionable alternative to lawns, I feel that my early days of professional gardening, which were spent doggedly challenging the norms of what a garden could be, are paying off at last and this fills me with good cheer. The term wildflower meadow has now come to mean a wide range of things to many people and has moved away from its original meaning of a semi-natural pasture with native wild flowers. A meadow now can mean anything from a wide range of naturalistic flower planting, including perennial pollinator borders, cornfield and other annual flowering displays, to even prairie-like plantings of non-native flowers and grasses. If you are considering moving from a lawn to a meadow it is important to be clear as to what type of meadow you are wanting. The use of mainly annual non-native seed mixes used in public areas by councils, while it is undoubtedly a huge improvement over mown grass verges, isn't strictly speaking a meadow. However, these mixes are very strong on colour through the summer months, and due to this are popular with humans and insects alike. For that reason alone, they are worth the space.

Why would you replace your lawn with a meadow? There are countless reasons from an ecological perspective, as long grass and flowers provide abundant habitat for a plethora of insects. I also consider meadows to be incredibly beautiful places and I love to watch a stand of grasses rippling in the wind and to have the opportunity to watch charms of goldfinches descending on the seed heads is simply a priceless treat for the eyes. There are other reasons too, perhaps it's just me, but lying on my back in long grass staring up at the sky takes me back to my childhood. I was a daydreamer and loved nothing better than immersing myself in nature. I was a builder of woodland dens and I had trees as friends. I lived in deepest suburbia but every chance I had, I got on my pushbike and escaped to the wilder edges of the estate. It was a joyful activity for me and I have wonderful memories of sunny summer days, listening to grasshoppers and watching the clouds drift by as I plotted my world dominion. Now, as an adult, I do it far less often than when I was a kid, but I do still take the time if I can. It feels like a guilty pleasure these days, squeezed into a busy working life, but then there are occasionally those amazing early summer days which are just too delicious not to take advantage of. It enables me to take five minutes just for myself. As I get older, I realise that we spend too much time dashing between jobs, staring at our phones and rarely take time to be fully present and grateful for those days which are so gorgeous they lift our souls and still our busy minds. I heartily recommend that you begin to sneak these precious moments into your life. If you do decide to grow a meadow or know one where you can indulge yourself, please take a moment to lie on the ground with your head in the long grass. Feel the sun on your face and be dazzled by the piercing blue of a summer sky. Breathe deeply and feel your body supported by the earth, as you allow your stresses and tension to sink down into the ground. Take a moment to just be and enjoy the sensation of a different perspective being immersed in nature. When you are ready, get up slowly and go back to your day and do let me know if this doesn't beat pushing a mower back and forth.

Meadow mania

The classic British hay meadows are a thing of great charm and something which in days past were a common sight in agricultural settings. Nostalgia, however, has been pushed aside and the economics of modern farming have made them into a relatively rare habitat in the countryside. Recreating these in a garden setting is of course possible, although these are prone to difficulties, especially on nutrient-rich soils, where, rather than the delicate flowers we hope for, strong-growing grasses and weeds tend to dominate. Poor soils and careful management can result in a successful native flower meadow and there are a couple of ways of establishing one in a garden. The first consideration is to choose this approach if you have a patch of poor land or a lawn which has been unimproved for many years, with the grass clippings removed and no fertiliser or weed killers applied. Initially, it is often best to simply change the management and stop mowing, to see what happens. You may be surprised as to what pops up. Some of the best mini meadows I have seen have been as a result of simply stopping mowing and allowing things to arrive of their own accord and I have even seen orchids appear in the most unlikely of places.

If you have a garden where the lawn has been fairly recently laid with either turf or seed, then it is highly likely that your lawn will consist predominantly of ryegrass. This is a shame. Rye is the most used species in lawns as it is hard wearing and tolerant of compaction. Unfortunately, it is one of the most boring grasses in flower, unlike a lot of our other native grasses which are delicately beautiful in their flowering. Rye also has the tendency to grow tall and fall over, especially after rain, making it a problem in that it then tends to swamp out other flowering plants as well as making it difficult to cut at the end of the season. If the grasses stay relatively low even when flowering, but the floral component is species poor, then the addition of wild flower plug plants is probably the best option. You can grow your own wild flowers from seed and grow them on in small pots until the autumn, when the grass can be cut short and the plants popped into the turf. Alternatively, there are a number of specialist plant nurseries who can supply a wide range of different native species for all types of soil and microclimates. The other route to establishing a native meadow is to remove the existing turf or other vegetation and seed the entire area in either autumn or spring. If your soils are rich then grasses have a tendency to dominate, although the addition of a semi-parasitic plant called yellow rattle can help to prevent the grass from taking over. Yellow rattle seed needs to be very fresh and autumn sown. It is an annual plant which sets seed every year, attaching itself to the roots of grass. Old seed does not tend to germinate well and as such it can sometimes be difficult to establish. An annual cut and removal of grass is necessary, this usually taking place in late summer. Be aware that this can be quite a time-consuming job, making meadows of this type not an entirely low maintenance option. Finally, there are now a few companies who offer wildflower turf to buy. If you are building a garden from scratch and have the money to spend, then these are potentially a good idea. They don't come cheap, however, and a good deal of ground preparation is advised first. Adding a layer of nutrient-poor subsoil, or even crushed building waste over any high-nutrient soils before laying the turf can be a good way of keeping the diversity high and the growth levels low.

The colourful, flower-rich, annual strips which have become more common in public areas are a simple way to achieve a meadow effect, especially if colour is high on your list of essential attributes. These can be based on native plants, such as those which used to be common in cornfields, for example, poppies, cornflowers, corncockle and the like. There are also plenty of bespoke seed mixes available on the market now that offer a longer flowering period and wider range of colour and flower types, although most of these are not strictly native to the UK. These seed mixes require a weed-free, well-cultivated soil. This is often achieved in public areas by applying a broad-spectrum herbicide and then rotavating the land before sowing the seed. This is not really in the spirit of alchemical gardening, due to the adverse effects on the soil and surrounding ecosystems. You could still use these if you are prepared to weed and rake the soil by hand every spring and buy new seed to sow. Disappointingly, many people do not realise that this is a requirement for this style of planting and I have known some folks who sow these seed mixes on top of an established lawn and are disheartened when this fails to achieve the result they had hoped for. This is particularly common with poppy seed too, as all too frequently people think that they will grow fine in long grass, despite this not being their preferred habitat.

Prairie planting is a term which has predominantly been used in the USA since it is a native habitat there. It has become popular as a style of planting as it relies mainly on perennial plants and grasses planted together as a matrix. It can look very effective, especially on a large scale and there are a number of garden designers who use this style to wonderful effect. As a meadow type of planting, it can be used extremely successfully in a domestic garden setting, although it does require a good plant knowledge to choose the types of plants which thrive in this style of planting. They do tend to resemble flower borders rather than meadows, so think carefully about where you would grow such planting, as in a small garden, it could look a little bit too dominant. It can be very low maintenance, once established, and although the flowering period tends to be peaking during the summer months, it is easy enough to underplant with spring bulbs to extend the season of interest. The other benefit of this style of planting is that it stands up well through the winter months, creating a multistructural layer of stems and seed heads, which offer great hibernation options for insects as well as a variety of seeds for birds. Prairie planting really needs to be planned in advance and initially planted into a weed-free border, although of course this can be achieved by no-dig methods of sheet mulching an area first and planting into that. It is tolerant of all types of soil, so if you have a nutrient-rich, heavy clay soil in your garden, then this might be your best option if you fancy something a bit wild and meadow-like.

The final option for meadow-type planting is to introduce plants into an already established lawn, but choose perennial plants which are robust enough to be happily grown in grass, with all the competition which this causes. Because most of the native wild flowers we associate with meadows are, in fact, stress tolerators, due to their ability to survive an annual hay cut as well as grazing by animals following that, they're often not suitable choices for areas where the grass species are competitive in habit. Luckily, there are plenty of both native and non-native flowers which will thrive, many of them are often cultivated varieties of plants which normally grow under similar conditions and share the same competitive traits. Planting bulbs into established grass is an easy way to begin to get some colour and interest and there is a wide range of suitable species from crocus, daffodils – of which there are literally thousands of varieties to choose from – *Camassia* and snakes' head fritillaries among others. This gives you a head start and a reason not to cut the grass until the leaves of these bulbs have died back. Then you can either introduce a few wild natives or choose some cultivated varieties of wildings, such as *Primulas*, hardy *Geranium*s, scabious, ox-eye daisies, yarrow – which comes now in lots of different colours – and even *Alchemilla*, as a reminder of what we are experimenting for. All of these plants and many more are suitable and robust enough to hold their own among grasses and don't mind being cut back hard at the end of summer.

Permaculture principle: Integrate rather than segregate

This permaculture principle is a plea for encouraging a greater mix of diversity in all types of communities. Just as plants work better and are healthier and more resilient when they're not grown as monocultures, then people too respond best when they work together as a group. We are far stronger together than we are apart and co-operation rather than competition is the best way for us all to thrive. We can learn this from the way that plants and fungi co-operate in order to fulfil the needs that they are unable to supply themselves. Trees grow more successfully when they team up with mycorrhizal fungi below ground, as this effectively increases the extent of their root systems as well as allowing some form of basic communication to take place between individuals of the same species in an area. This collaboration also enables trees to support and provide for any member of their arboreal community who are sick or ailing, by sending nutrients and water to each other when required.

In gardening, this principle is useful when we are contemplating growing plants together in a border, or else thinking of growing vegetables in our garden. This encourages us to mix up the different aspects of a garden; for example, growing flowers next to your vegetables, rather like the idea of companion planting, where some plants appear to offer benefits to others around them, whether this is due to them being nitrogen-fixing species, such as peas and beans, or perhaps they attract beneficial insects, such as pollinators or can act to distract the more problematic insects such as aphids.

A prime example of plants being mixed up in a small area, offering both beauty and useful products from one plot, is the old-fashioned cottage garden or the more ornamental potager, which was a formal layout of mixed food and flowers grown together. This way of growing is now often referred to as polyculture, where a variety of food plants are grown together, rather than in monoculture rows or blocks. Some people find that done carefully it enables you to be able to grow more vegetables within the space you have, making it much more productive. It's one that I heartily encourage everyone to try again.

If you are wanting to grow your own fruit and vegetables, it is entirely possible to incorporate food plants into your natural garden without needing to make a specific space for them. Some vegetables are highly ornamental, such as chard, lettuce and kale, particularly the coloured-leaved varieties, and even courgettes or pumpkins. Peas and beans can easily be grown up tepees or trellis in the ornamental garden and most people passing by wouldn't even consider that they were food plants. It is possible to buy broad beans that have beautiful purple flowers; even some root crops such as carrot can be highly decorative. There are also plenty of plants that we habitually grow as ornamentals which are also edible. Examples of these are day lilies (*Hemerocallis*), which have edible flowers which can be added to salads for a colourful snack, and *Hosta*s, whose newly emerging leaf spikes taste like asparagus and are apparently excellent steamed or gently fried in butter. Many of the old cottage garden flowers can also be eaten: tiny violas; old-fashioned marigolds; and nasturtiums, whose flowers, leaves and unripe seeds all pack a peppery punch when added to meals. The other advantage to growing vegetables mixed in with your flowers is that pests can find it harder to track them down.

Of course, there are many other ways to introduce vegetables and fruit into the garden; food can be easily grown in pots, raised beds and all manner of re-purposed containers. If you are lucky enough to have sufficient space to have a dedicated vegetable plot then there are plenty of ways that you can manage this in a nature-friendly way. The standard approach to vegetable growing is one which I struggle with, the uniformity, the suggestion that we need to dig and rotavate and fertilise and the almost obsessive ideas of tidiness, all make me a bit sad. While it is possible to grow vegetables very successfully in a no-dig way, the approach still tends to be one of 'show garden' neatness which is completely unnecessary. I often think that this enduring vision of the perfect vegetable plot puts a lot of people off growing their own food. Anyone who doesn't achieve this ridiculously high standard is seen to have failed to 'keep on top' of everything and plenty of beginner gardeners give up at this first hurdle.

No-dig vegetable gardening works by layering organic matter on the undisturbed ground and planting into that. It is claimed that this is the best way to avoid weeds but, in reality, unless we are master composters who never add seeding weeds to the pile, or who manage to get the temperature hot enough to kill weed seeds throughout, then this is likely to be a bit of a myth. Some people use bought-in multipurpose compost for layering on the soil, but personally I think this is not only a very expensive way of growing vegetables, but that the carbon footprint of gardening in this way far exceeds the benefits of home growing, although it will, of course, be weed free.

As we have previously discovered, it is not just organic matter which creates soil fertility, but the presence of plants. Organic matter is a key component, but it is the plants themselves which are able to maintain that fertility in the soil. Vegetables, being mainly annual short-lived plants are slightly problematic in that they don't stay in situ very long and nature will always be keen to replace any harvested vegetables with other plants to keep the system stable. During the main growing season in spring and summer, this is easy enough for the gardener to achieve, simply by planting seeds or small plants to take over once something has been cropped. As we approach the autumn and winter, this becomes ever more difficult to do.

Cover crops and green manures are one way of dealing with this problem of not leaving soil bare. The other way, which I prefer, is to allow nature to supply the cover crops for you. You might call them weeds, but let's face it, they all fulfil the same role as far as nature is concerned. If an area isn't currently being used for anything, then allowing a few weeds to grow is the best option for maintaining fertility in the soil. Once you need the area back again, then you can simply remove the weeds and add them to the compost pile, or else cover them with a thick layer of organic matter to smother them. This latter approach is particularly useful towards the end of winter, when a layer of cardboard and compost or woodchip is a really quick way of getting ready for spring planting. Areas should only ever be cleared as they are needed. Attempting to keep the entire vegetable plot weed free is not only a lot of work for the gardener, but it is bad for the soil. This can be avoided by changing your mind set from thinking it looks messy and untidy to being much more accepting of native ground cover crops, or, in other words, being tolerant of a few weeds. Obviously, I am not suggesting that you let your weeds self-seed everywhere, making a long-term problem for yourself, or letting highly competitive species completely take over, but I am suggesting that a bit of grass, a few dandelions and groundsel are fine. If you do have invasive weeds such as ground elder, then I suggest that growing annual vegetables in that space is going to be far more work than is practical and perhaps you might need to reconsider and try container growing instead.

Growing in containers is a useful way to supplement your weekly shop, but it is a potentially time-consuming method of vegetable growing. The larger the pot or container, the easier it will be, but keeping on top of watering and ensuring there is sufficient fertility to continuously take crops can be difficult. Using ordinary garden soil, rather than multipurpose compost can help, as it tends not to dry out as quickly and is able to retain fertility a little easier. However, if you love the flavour of freshly plucked peas straight from the pod or the first boiling of new potatoes in the spring, then there is no reason not to grow such things in containers, if this is your only option. Having a few herbs in a pot by the back door or in a window box is an excellent way to grow your own and I highly recommend this, even if you think that you don't have time for anything else more complicated.

Food forests

A food forest or forest garden is a way of growing trees, shrubs, climbers and herbaceous perennial plants as a low-maintenance and self-sustaining mixed planting. It is designed to emulate natural woodland ecosystems in that it mimics the layers of planting which would naturally be found in the wild, but it replaces non-edible plants with food crops. This method of gardening is commonplace in tropical countries and is starting to gain popularity in western temperate countries too. Based on layers of vegetation, it starts with an over-storey of (usually) fruit trees. Below this canopy is a layer of shrubs, such as berries, then herbaceous perennial plants like sorrel or asparagus. There can be groundcover plants like alpine strawberry which will fill the spaces at ground level and finally there are climbers, such as kiwi-fruit or even brambles.

The idea is that this type of planting can provide some of your food requirements close at hand without very much input from the gardener once established, other than picking and processing the food. As a way of supplementing your diet, this is an excellent approach to use, although this doesn't take account of the fact that the majority of our most frequently eaten food plants are, in fact, annuals. If you were considering trying to be more self-reliant in growing your own food, then clearly a combination of the more traditional vegetable garden in conjunction with a forest garden would be your best option. However, if you simply wanted to produce a bit more of your own food, then forest gardening can be an excellent route to doing this, without a lot of effort.

A forest garden is a lovely way to combine both productivity and wildness into your plot. It is an efficient use of space, as there is capacity to cram an impressive number and variety of useful plants in there. Quite a number of suitable plants are also wildlife friendly. Growing in this manner can mean that you might be happy to share some of your harvest with the wild creatures who share your garden, as it can be a very productive way to grow. There can also be the bonus of having other useful harvests from your forest garden, such as material for composting, stakes and pea sticks for the rest of the garden; some people even tap birch trees, collect pine pollen and gather nettle fibres for spinning. Once you begin to investigate the ways of increasing your yield from a forest garden, the results can be astounding.

June arrived, bustling in like a diva, demanding admiration and deference. I had barely registered the gentle presence of May before she shimmied out again, leaving a trail of blossom in her wake. The garden is in full flow – flamboyant and unapologetic. Flower after flower appear to join the throng in a dizzying parade of colour, scent and lush growth. As I wander around the garden, particularly in the early hours of the morning, I feel a certain pride in my collaboration with nature in my plot. The buttercup-resplendent grass field provides a seamless backdrop to the wild perennial border, blurring the edges between natural and cultivated. The air smells of summer, sweetly fragrant, of warm earth and resinous tree sap, roses and sweet lilies in pots by the door.

No need now, for a torch to light the last dog walk of the evening before bed. Three weeks until the solstice and the days start early and stretch luxuriously into gentle soft evenings. While it's still chilly at night, even with a jumper on, the evenings are full of magic and I am unable to ignore them and stay inside. The skies over the garden are thick with midges, the swallows gyrate in a feeding frenzy, petering out just as the bats take over after the sun slips out of view, leaving behind layers of tangerine and apricot-coloured clouds. I sit for a while on the bench near the pond, reflecting on the day, my scalp itching with the bites of the tiny bloodsuckers, before I retreat, defeated, back inside to light a small fire in the stove, these northern nights still warrant the effort.

I contemplate what it means to belong to somewhere. I'm still learning about what it is which binds us to a place. Earthbound. We are bound to the earth and for it eventually, too. This garden, which has tested me both horticulturally and personally, has seeped into my bones without me realising. I am more than superficially acquainted with this small patch of land now and still it has much to teach me. I have examined my role as a curator and artistic director of the plants I have introduced to the garden and, despite my years of experience, there are some things which haven't worked out as I had imagined. Not wanting to impose my will too strongly, I have watched carefully as the natural ebb and flow of floral highlights weave themselves around the place.

I think about the sheep which appear from time to time, wandering down from the moor to see what I am doing and wonder how they know where they belong. Without clear boundaries, no borders or fences to dictate their homeland, they never seem to become lost in the landscape. We describe these wily moorland creatures as being hefted to the land, a knowledge which is passed down through the generations and absorbed by each generation. It has been suggested that the habits acquired by a creature can be passed down to their young, without the need to teach them, a sort of genetic transference. Perhaps this is what we mean when we think of where our roots are, where we belong. My great grandparents were country folk, farm workers mainly, yet their offspring moved into the industrial towns of the north to work down the coal mines, and my own parents were happy enough living in an industrial town. Yet every weekend, we escaped into the rural edges of town to walk, forage for wild food and spend time in the woods and fields. So it should come as no surprise that I am drawn to wild places and have chosen to live in a remote place away from modern society and its conveniences.

Invitations to celebrate the season

- Consider letting your grass grow long by retiring the mower for a few weeks, even just a little patch can make a difference for wildlife. If you don't have a lawn, why not write to your local council and ask them to stop mowing for the month of May (and beyond) and see what wild flowers pop up.

- Collect some elderflower blossoms and consider making some elderflower champagne or cordial. There are lots of recipes on the internet and it makes a delicious change from alcohol or sugary fizzy drinks.

- Put up some insect hotels or bee boxes, or have a go at making them yourself. They come in all sorts of designs and make an interesting addition to any garden, as well as providing essential homes and habitats for invertebrates.

- Make yourself a flower crown. Find a nice sunny place, where daisies grow and make yourself a daisy chain. You might not have done this since you were a child, but indulge yourself and spend a pleasant half hour or so, picking and threading these lovely flowers together. Even better, find a child, if you don't have one of your own and teach them how to make them for themselves. Wear your flowers with pride.

CHAPTER EIGHT:

Litha: The Summer Solstice

I awoke just as it was getting light, around a quarter to four and snoozed until half past. While it would have been so easy to roll over and go back to sleep, I figured that if you are going to get up early once a year to watch the sun rise, then this was the very best day to do it. It was worth the effort. I felt as though I was the only human on the planet, although the birds were very much in evidence and I watched a family of roe deer in the distance, picking their way along the field at the edge of the woodland. By mid-afternoon the sun was blazing down, hot and fierce. I had noticed the blackbirds on the currant bushes that morning when everything was so still; a constant conveyor of ripe berries being carried away in eager beaks. There was nothing for it other than to harvest a few for myself before they all disappeared. Luckily, it was a perfect sitting-down job, made for a day such as this, after a very early start, which I was trying not to regret due to my tiredness. A sudden rustling behind me gave away the presence of a song thrush, caught in the act of brazenly helping itself to berries from the adjacent bush. Cross, I stood up and clapped my hands, yet despite my protestations it remained gulping down the berries even faster. It flew off into the hawthorn as I approached it, so I returned to the job in hand. The thrush hopped up on to the highest branch and sang, a haunting lyrical refrain, making my heart soften enough to allow it rejoin me in the blackcurrant harvest. I smiled. Such a simple task, made so delightful by kicking off my shoes and socks, watching my wild kin and taking my time in a sun-drenched moment.

The last few weeks have been gloriously hot. Sun-soaked and colour-saturated with the bluest of skies. The land is sun-baked hard and cracking, the grasses bleached and dry. Like the land, I too am turning brown and blond in the relentless sun. The extended midsummer days can leave me weary as I try to take full advantage of the long sun-soaked hours, so I contemplate the option of the siesta, in order to conserve energy and avoid the heat of the day. I find myself needing to water new plantings in the vegetable plot, as well as the young trees and shrubs I planted through the winter months. I try to water heavily yet infrequently, and I learn that those plants which I took the time to mulch with woodchips, cardboard or compost are faring much better for having a layer of organic material acting as insulation from the heat of the sun as well as reducing evaporation of water from the soil surface.

The garden is perhaps at its most voluptuous right now and the insects are in heaven with the range and diversity of flowers on offer to them. It is peak growing time, as the days are so long and although it doesn't seem long since I was wishing for everything to grow, now it just feels unstoppable. The sides of the roads haven't been cut back yet, perhaps a benefit of council spending cuts this year and the wild flowers nod and wave as I drive past them. My favourite wild things at the moment are the umbellifers, whose spindrift of white frothy flowers are buoyant on a billowing sea of green. I tell myself that I will encourage more of these types of plants in my own garden, as they are not only fabulous when in full bloom, but they also leave the most elegant of plant skeletons to provide interest throughout the winter months, as well as providing vital hibernation places for invertebrates.

Water

I used to think that ponds were for people with big gardens and that a pond was a bit of a luxury item, something I couldn't really justify. Then one day I decided to say yes to an old sand pit that my friend was getting rid of, I sunk it into the ground in the garden of my rented house and filled it with water and pebbles. Within a week, I was captivated. Pond skaters had arrived and there was a queue of birds lining up to drink and bathe in it. Another friend gave me some water-loving plants from her own pond and another few weeks later, I had a startling blue damselfly investigating, zipping back and forth like a tiny biplane. Although I have since been through a series of house moves, I now always try to create some form of watery habitat, as one of the very best ways to increase the diversity of wildlife that visit or make a home in your garden is to introduce water.

From a purely selfish and human-centred point of view, I love my pond. It has only been in place a couple of years, but it has settled into a valuable habitat for wild creatures and a source of wonder and a calming influence for me. On days which are warm enough to sit outside for any length of time, my favourite place is next to the pond. I find it simultaneously soothing when my mind is full of chatter and endlessly fascinating when my mind is blank and I need some inspiration. It isn't very large, but I have dragonflies and damselflies visiting and laying their eggs in it, frogs of course have discovered it and there are countless tiny creatures which live within it, none of which I have introduced. From great diving beetles to pond skaters, I often wonder how on earth these aquatic insects arrive here. It certainly confirms the truth of the old adage regarding wildlife habitats, that if you build it, they will come. I have also built a log pile close by the pond and underneath some shrubs, to fulfil the requirements of somewhere to hibernate for those beings who, rather sensibly in my opinion, choose to spend winter asleep under cover. Log piles can be made to look like an intentional feature in the garden, they don't have to resemble a pile of twigs that you forgot to take to the tip. If you can, try to choose wood which will make a stable and decorative statement in the garden, surround it with ferns or marginal pond plants and soon you will attract plenty of creatures which will love the improvements to the neighbourhood.

From a more aesthetic gardening perspective, adding water to the garden adds a layer of interest and enables you to grow a wider range of plants than you would otherwise be able to. Water has the innate ability to reflect light, so the positioning of the water needs to be carefully thought through, so it can be in a place where you are likely to appreciate the ripples over water on a breezy day or marvel at the reflection of the sky in all its mutable moods, from salmon-pink-tinted sunsets to towering clouds and bright blue skies. Things to think about when putting water into the garden are: where to place it for best effect and fewest problems; how to ensure the safety of other garden users, whether these are young children or young birds and mammals; and, finally, how large are you able to go – do you have the energy to dig a large pond, or are you in rented accommodation and just want something small and simple? A buried bucket or a half barrel make interesting water features, especially when planted around with water-loving, sympathetic plants.

From a wildlife perspective, it is better if your pond is situated in a sunny place. Ideally, avoid having them too close to deciduous trees, as removing the leaves in autumn and winter is a tiresome and stinky task. A pond, if you are going to make one, should be as large as you have space for. As a rule of thumb, the larger the body of water, the more stable the water temperature will be and this has the benefit of reducing the likelihood of algae build-up as well as stopping the pond freezing solid in cold winters. Once you have marked out where you want your pond, it is time to start digging – one of the very few times that I will be asking you to do this! It is always advisable to have a shallow end to a pond with a gentle gradient – a kind of pebble beach, if you like – which will enable access into and out of the water for any hapless creatures who might fall in. The shallows are also a favourite place for tadpoles to gather and sun themselves on sunny spring days and for birds to have a bath and preen themselves. One day, while sitting and drinking tea with a customer in the garden I had designed for her, we remarked on how quickly the pond had settled in and become a lovely feature. We sat still, in silent witness, as a blackbird hopped down for a bath in the stony shallows, seemly oblivious to our presence. Imagine our horror then, as the blackbird began to devour a number of fat healthy tadpoles that were also gathered there, the bird flying off with a still-wriggling specimen in his bright-yellow beak, presumably to feed his mate or chicks with. A salutary tale in the complexity of the food web within nature and how everything is interlinked.

Water has an ability to make a garden seem much larger and brighter. Still water invites the sky down to ground level. It acts like a mirror and suggests that you spend some time imitating the water, in reflecting on what is around you. The ripples add to the illusion, as it distorts these reflected images at the slightest breeze on the surface, creating an otherworldly vision of the trees and buildings around. There are all sorts of options for adding fountains or rills and making a real feature out of water. These are entirely the choice of the gardener and the sound of running water is known to calm the mind and encourage a more relaxed state. However, I feel that this potentially strays into being too human centred and that a still pond, with natural planting around the margins is almost certainly the best option for wildlife.

It's early July, the weather is glorious and I find myself working from home. My heart dearly wants to be in the garden, but my brain tells me I have to work, as I have deadlines to fulfil. I find myself alternating between being inside and finding excuses to go outdoors, not the most productive mindset, but one which seems to offer the most acceptable compromise. A dragonfly zooms in while I am sitting on the bench next to my small pond, drinking a coffee and taking a mindful five minutes away from the computer screen. I had been sitting with my eyes closed, concentrating on breathing when I heard the whirring wings zip, distractingly close, past my head. I cannot help but open my eyes to take a closer look and I realise that it has landed right next to me on the bench. Looking like something from the time of dinosaurs, I am amazed when it turns its head, seemingly to look more closely at me too. It's a large insect, strikingly striped in black and yellow with a determined air about it as it goes about its business. It lifts off again and skims above the water level a few more times, before flying off once more. I discover, on returning to the laptop, that it was golden ringed dragonfly, not a particularly rare specimen, but a very special encounter for me. I also learn that in many cultures dragonflies are considered to be symbols of good luck and hope, and that a visit from a dragonfly can be a sign of moving beyond our self-imposed limitations that limit our personal growth and ability to change. You might not believe in the symbolism of animals, and I do fall into that sceptical category, yet as I was mentally working towards imagining a new future for myself, I was more than happy to take that particular message on board.

Water in the garden reminds us of the dynamic flows which take place throughout all natural systems. Flow and movement are essential aspects of both gardens and life, a deep knowing that nothing is static and that this change and uncertainty brings beauty along with it. Sitting by water allows us to appreciate reflection, the ability to look up without actually doing so. Reflecting is a gentle pastime, one which might, on occasion, bring a sense of melancholy but also highlights and illuminates the little world we inhabit with sparkles of lightness, an intense perspective, which can jolt and jiggle us out of our routines and ruts.

Permaculture principle: Use edges and value the marginals

This permaculture principle encourages us to explore having a range of different habitats within the garden. Edges are the point where two things meet. In the case of ecosystems, the edges are frequently the most diverse as far as species are concerned, as they overlap two different niches or environments. In nature, this overlap of two types of ecosystem can offer a rich and rewarding habitat for a large and varied population of creatures, much more so than if we simply looked at the two separately and independently. Living life on the edge has never been so exciting. In the garden, if we can create a number of different habitats, from ponds, to meadows and shady log piles, the more places we have where these different areas encounter each other, the more likely it is that wildlife can find a suitable home. It also allows us to make more of the different spaces within our gardens, ensuring that there is beauty and interest throughout.

This is a very useful thing to consider, especially in the smaller garden where it is likely that your entire garden feels as though it is a series of edges, with not much in the middle. Fences and walls are perfect for some vertical gardening, *Clematis* is beautiful and is great for small nesting birds; *Pyracantha* is a very effective and spiky barrier, evergreen, with masses of creamy-white flowers in early summer followed by prolific bunches of berries which last well into the winter. Fruit trees can be grown on dwarfing rootstocks and trained against walls which will hold the heat and allow the fruit to ripen sooner than if they were growing on a standard tree.

Marginal land in farming is that which is considered to be the least productive and requiring the most work and external inputs in order to achieve a harvest, such as hilly upland regions or areas with difficult microclimates. In a domestic garden setting, marginal land is similarly challenged, although usually due to deep shade, such as on the northern side of a house, or perhaps because the conditions are difficult due to poor soil, especially in newly built properties, where the building contractors are renowned for burying rubble and other building waste and covering it up with a thin layer of imported topsoil. This principle invites you to look at whether you can work with what you have, rather than trying to improve the garden to fit in with the plants you wanted to grow. For instance, growing a wildflower meadow, especially using native species, will be considerably easier and more successful on poor, thin soils, rather than trying the same on deep nutrient-rich clay soils. You may, however, find that your beloved *Dahlias* won't do so well in similar conditions. Equally, trees and hedges are often considered to offer problems when it comes to gardening, due to their competition for soil moisture, nutrients and light conditions. Rather than deciding to get rid of what you already have, consider planting a range of shade- and drought-tolerant plants which will thrive under these circumstances.

Rewilding

Returning to the garden, I decide that I am going to give up on maintaining one of the borders I had planted. It was one of the earlier spaces that I furnished with plants, a crazy mixture of species which had languished in pots for too long after being brought from my last garden; as such it became a bit of a mish-mash and I became bored with trying to govern the unruly inhabitants. I had planted a wide range of plants with very differing personalities and it wasn't working out too well. The area was full of couch grass which, no matter how much I tried to control it, always seemed to sneak back into the border while my back was turned. Rather than continue to try and referee the mayhem which had ensued, I decided in the interests of science to leave them to their own devices to see what would happen. Not surprisingly, several of the plants took over the space, others still appeared to migrate to areas which suited them better and gradually the border became a kind of cultivated meadow, with a wild edge to it. There are some woody plants in there, a witch hazel (*Hamamelis*), which will eventually dominate the area and hopefully change the growing conditions sufficiently for the snowdrops and cyclamen I had planted to hold their own among the grass. The thing with gardening is that you never stop learning, as long as you are able to acknowledge your mistakes and admit that nature probably knew what was best for this part of the garden.

I contemplate the concept of rewilding from the viewpoint of a garden and wonder if it is an oxymoron. We need to examine what it is that defines a garden and ask why we can't let the natural world take over these spaces and go completely wild? Wikipedia, my initial go-to source for pretty much everything on the internet, gives the clear and concise definition that 'a garden is a planned space, usually outdoors, set aside for the display, cultivation, or enjoyment of plants and other forms of nature, as an ideal setting for social or solitary human life. The single feature identifying even the wildest wild garden is control.' Such a statement is unequivocal in its assumption that for a space to be considered a garden, the human hand must be evident in its planning and maintenance. Personally, I believe that people think rather too highly of themselves in this context, but it is true that all gardens, natural or otherwise have some degree of human input in their creation. Therefore, is it even possible to rewild a garden and still consider it to be a garden and if so, what do we mean by rewilding?

Wild or messy?

Who on earth was it who decided that everything had to be so tidy? This obsession with neatness has even started to influence our perception of more natural spaces in the countryside beyond our gardens. So many public open spaces are now treated in the same way as urban gardens. The roadside verges which used to be full of wild flowers are now regularly mown throughout the summer months, to keep everything looking tidy, or sprayed with selective herbicides to keep 'weeds' from spreading into agriculture. Farmers' field hedgerows are flailed to resemble suburban garden hedges, orderly and neat, ultimately robbing our bird populations of their winter food store by removing berries before they can be eaten. By spraying herbicides, the soil is left bare instead of allowing a few weeds to establish, and we find ourselves striving to maintain some order on the abundance that nature will produce given the chance. The eradication of these patches of wildness, both in our gardens and our wider communities, have produced a depleted and less sustaining environment, for ourselves, our imaginations and the precious wildlife we share our land with.

Rewilding has really captured the imagination of the wider public in recent times. It has become a commonly used term, due to some high-profile experiments in returning land to nature by means of stopping the farming of unprofitable land in the conventional manner and allowing nature to progress through a series of stages of natural regeneration. While the concept was originally conceived to encapsulate the methods of ecosystem restoration by allowing plant succession to take place without any human intervention, it has clearly grown to encompass much more than this. The word 'rewilding' has now become a description covering a wide number of nature-friendly approaches, from a 'what if we just leave it alone' angle to a swathe of human interventions as diverse as creating wildflower meadows, introducing free ranging and low-density grazing animals, digging new ponds or even just tree planting. The rewilding movement has even expanded to encouraging people to spend more time in touch with nature, whether this is in a countryside setting, or even by simply growing houseplants. I would like to take a closer look at rewilding from a purely gardening perspective and see how these ideas might be useful to the small-scale grower and what the advantages could be in providing better habitats for both wild life and humans. In some ways, the use of rewilding techniques is not entirely appropriate for a garden setting, but there are definitely aspects which are useful in discovering the alchemy of your garden and making it much more wildlife friendly.

Rewilding is, in some circles, a controversial method of nature conservation, as many people believe that 'letting land go back to nature' will just create an unsightly and weedy mess and that it is a waste of good productive land. While it is true that there is a need for the UK to be able to supply good and nutritious food for the population, there is an equally important requirement for taking a long hard look at what modern agriculture is actually delivering. The rewilding movement has at least made this conversation more acceptable. Rewilding isn't suitable for all land, but it can be an excellent use of land which is too marginal and unproductive for conventional farming methods and it offers a wide range of other benefits such as climate change mitigation, flood prevention and providing diverse open spaces to benefit human populations while attempting to reverse biodiversity losses of native flora and fauna.

Rewilding is, therefore, a term which is generally regarded as letting land revert to natural processes. In this case, the first plants which will often take advantage of a lack of human management will often be those which we consider to be weeds. This is far from being a static outcome as rewilding is a dynamic process which changes considerably over time. Left to their own devices, these weeds would then become overtaken by more woody plants, initially species which we refer to as scrub, mainly smaller-growing shrubs, before they in turn are succeeded by trees as the land returns to woodland. This is what ecologists call succession, or the transition over a period of time, that changes which types of vegetation become dominant in a landscape. In the UK, this process was thought to have meant that originally we were a much more wooded country and that the majority of land was covered by trees. While this is in part the case, as we did used to have a lot more woodland, it appears that a more patchwork landscape existed, comprising a mix of meadow, scrub and trees. This formed a mosaic of overlapping habitats, rich in wildlife.

This patchwork of different environments came about by the interventions of not only human behaviour but also the actions of wild animals, especially herbivores. From browsing deer to rootling wild boar, these animals had an impact on the habitats they lived in, creating areas of flower-rich meadows, patches of scrub – kept low by animal action – and areas of woodland, from the old and established to new and emerging areas of young saplings. These diverse areas were constantly changing, dynamic and probably responded to alterations in climate, extreme weather events and, of course, the actions of human settlers and their domesticated beasts.

In large rewilding projects on farmland, such as that at Knepp, which was the first major lowland rewilding project in England, grazing and browsing animals with wild rather than domesticated instincts were deliberately introduced to fulfil these essential interventions which allow this diverse habitat to exist. Historically, there was probably much more small-scale farming and subsistence growing which added to this mix. Over time, the quintessential British rural landscape of fields, hedges, copses and wood pasture evolved to become an almost formalised version of the wilder mix of different habitats. The removal of hedgerows in the 1970s to make larger fields and the loss of small woodlands and the draining of wet areas has led to a landscape which lacks the variety of habitat required as well as the connectivity between habitats to ensure a good healthy wildlife population. By allowing these natural processes to take place, the food web improves for a wide range of creatures. Permitting a few sections of land to revert to more natural vegetation types is a great way to turn the tables on the losses we have witnessed due to industrial agricultural techniques and is probably the most effective way of balancing the need for wild habitats as well as food production. As we are coming from a very depleted baseline, any improvement can be beneficial.

Whether rewilding is a suitable approach for domestic gardens is questionable, particularly as people will want to gain pleasure from spending time in them, cultivating favourite flowers and producing herbs and vegetables for their own use. Few people have the benefit of owning sufficiently large gardens to be able to fulfil all their needs while also allowing rewilding to take place. However, at a purely gardening level, our own interventions as gardeners can allow for a greater mix of habitats, even if we are unable to wholly embrace a rewilding concept. This puts the gardener as the keystone species that affects the outcome of any rewilding experiments. The key thing to remember is that at a domestic level, whether you are gardening purely for wildlife, or for flowers or food, you will probably be planting a much wider range of plant species than would naturally occur in the wild. This is actually an added bonus for wildlife, as it has the capacity to extend the flowering period considerably, attracting a healthy population of insects to feed on the nectar and pollen available. The insects and subsequently the seed heads of these plants will, in turn, feed a wide range of wild birds, all adding to the biodiversity in your garden space.

An individual garden doesn't have to offer the same types and range of habitat as that of a rewilded landscape. It is clearly not going to be practical to achieve, notwithstanding that most people's gardens are of course far too small to consider trying to cram so much in. Since the larger the individual habitat, the more resilient its associated population of wildlife is going to be, then if you simply fancy growing a wild flower meadow or even just a bee-friendly flower border, then this is going to be fine. As I suggested earlier, it is through joining together the tiny fragments of habitat in our gardens that we can make a wonderfully varied patchwork of designed wildness. Hopefully, you will have a neighbour who prefers shrubs, perfect for birds to nest in and another who has a little wildlife pond and a log pile in a shady place beneath a tree. By working together, we can create a mosaic of beautiful and productive habitats, creating much more than if we were simply working in isolation. Ensuring that wild creatures are able to move between gardens is essential and providing small gaps in fences for hedgehogs to access, for example, will allow our individual efforts to be shared equally.

While this is only partially in the spirit of rewilding, the consideration of habitat creation for wildlife as an intrinsic aspect of the design with a more hands-off approach to gardening can be seen as a useful addition to a wilder landscape across the UK. Linking these areas by allowing the roadside verges to grow long and flower and only cutting hedgerows at the end of winter, allows these routes to be used as corridors for the movement of wild animals as well as humans.

Permaculture principle: Use and value diversity

This principle tells us that variety is the spice of life. Nothing in nature suggests that single species' systems are something to be aspired to. The more there is an assortment of organisms, the healthier the ecosystem will be. This works for human communities as well as plants, as in nature we are all more resilient when we can co-operate with many different people or creatures. We are always stronger together. Biodiversity allows us to be more resilient; groups of species working together encourage stability, security and a vested interest in maintaining a healthy environment as something all can benefit from. From a garden perspective, this encourages us to grow a wide variety of plants in our gardens; the value to ourselves and to wildlife, of plenty of assorted flowers and plants, is higher than simply using a restricted range.

There is a widely held opinion that a natural garden should only contain those plants which are native to that garden's specific country. The definition of a native plant is one which occurs naturally in a particular region or ecosystem and has not been introduced by humans. Native plants have an innate ability to thrive in the soils, climate and conditions in which they are found and have usually evolved alongside a wide range of other species, both plants and animals. In the UK, this means a fairly limited palette of wild things – those that were growing on these islands after the Ice Age. Although many of these native plants and flowers are beautiful, there is no need for we, as gardeners, to limit ourselves solely to these species. Including non-native plants allows us a much more exciting paint box to play in and a garden containing a variety of cultivated plants offers a wider range of habitats and niches for wildlife than a similar patch of land left to 'go wild' with just a few early appearing native species.

We are a month past the longest day now and a golden hue creeps across the landscape, matching the sun-kissed brown of my skin. The grasses have flowered and have ripened in the sun to the colour of cinder toffee, smelling sweet and dusty in the heat of the day. The background rhythm of insect life lulls me, the bass drone of bumblebees and the high-hat percussion of the grasshoppers set a trance-like cadence to the garden tasks at hand. It is mostly vegetable garden work which occupies my time, as there is nothing to do in the summer garden, apart from ensuring I take the time to appreciate it fully. I have creeping thistles in my vegetable plot and I eventually accept that I can't really leave them any longer, as they have become large and started to crowd out the brassicas. It is satisfying, if rather prickly, work, teasing the long white roots carefully out of the ground. I am content to leave the thistles in the field where we have planted trees. I notice that they seem to keep the grass at bay, which in turn allows the trees to establish quickly and more successfully. They have the added advantage of keeping the wild deer from browsing the young tree saplings, as well as emitting the most incredible sweet scent when they are in flower, attracting pollinators from all around. At the end of the year, the thistles' seed heads erupt in fluffy mountains of cloud-like down, which are rapidly devoured by huge flocks of finches.

Invitations to celebrate the season

- Walk barefoot. There is nothing more lovely than kicking off your shoes and walking barefoot in the garden. It allows you to feel the earth beneath your feet and helps you feel more relaxed and connected to nature. Be careful not to step on a foraging bee.

- Collect herbs from your garden to dry for use later in the winter. Herbs are best picked early in the day, once any dew has evaporated. Bundle them into small bunches and hang them up in the house, preferably near an open window, where the breeze can help them to dry more quickly. Once fully dried, store in a jar.

- Pick yourself a bunch of flowers from the garden to place on your table. Change the display regularly to echo the changing floral displays outside. Do you know the names of the flowers? It's a good way to learn them by admiring the different flowers close up.

CHAPTER NINE

Lammas

The first of the celebrations of harvest and abundance. This is one of my favourite times of year and this day, 1st August, also celebrates everything Yorkshire! I have been known on occasion to wear my father's flat cap and walk the whippet in the woods before heading home for a good strong cup of Yorkshire tea. Actually, in reality, I'm much more of an Earl Grey tea kind of lass, but perhaps this doesn't quite fit the humorous narrative as neatly. I always think that Lammas offers us the opportunity to pause briefly and express gratitude for summer beauty, grace and bounty. Those precious weeks of full summer following the solstice so frequently feel as though they slip through our hands faster than sand, as we work and play hard through the long days, to make the most of the glorious sun-filled days. Lammas is a nudge to stand still for a moment and absorb fully the blessings of summertime.

The harvests are indeed coming thick and fast. The runner beans have begun to crop and courgette mountain has started to become a problem as we run out of ideas for recipes which include that most ubiquitous of summer vegetables. Any social event sees me baking a cake to take, with secret courgette grated into it, in an attempt to share the abundance. Every Sunday, I pick a huge bunch of flowers from the garden to bring into the house. As I sit and eat my breakfast every morning, I try to name them all with their Latin 'Sunday names' as a reminder to myself that my brain cells need to be exercised too. Fatigue is a common theme of my days now with a chronic illness; this not only affects my physical energy levels but also my cognitive functioning as well. On those days when my head feels full of cotton wool and I am finding it difficult to remember what I did five minutes ago, never mind what I should be doing next, I find that writing down plant names to remember gives me a gentle mental workout as well as encouraging me to spend time admiring the tiny details and intricacies of flowers observed at close quarters.

Plant personalities

Selecting plants which work well together is as critical to creating alchemy in your garden as choosing people to throw a fabulous party with. It all comes down to personalities and preferences and ensuring that there won't be a terrible clash which ends up with half the people leaving early, while the remainder trash the house and annoy the neighbours. Let's face it, we have all been to those types of parties and I definitely know some gardens which have fallen into this category. In reality, it is these horticultural disagreements which are most likely to create chaos in the borders. Plants form their own tribes in the natural world and we will examine these different tribes and discover how they might not get along too well if they have to share their space with one another.

We frequently make mistakes by not looking at things from a plant's perspective. Plants are social beings. It is rare in nature to find a habitat which supports only one single type of plant species – diversity is the benchmark for a healthy environment. Like ourselves, plants prefer the company of others, but they also, like us, have strong preferences, both for what conditions they like to grow in and also which other plants that they like share that space with. Broadly speaking, there are three main types of plants and these types have individual characteristics, known as strategies, and these are the way in which plants are able to take advantage of different habitats and their specific conditions. Choosing garden plants just for their looks can be as disastrous as using the same criteria in human relationships – some sort of common ground and shared interests are always helpful too. Successful gardens are based on knowing your plants. If you are time poor and see gardening as a chore, then getting this element right is crucial to avoiding a mountain of work for yourself.

Permaculture principle: Creatively use and respond to change

This permaculture principle is essential when working closely with plants, as they teach us so much about the dynamic qualities of natural ecosystems and how these change, both by the season and over longer time periods. Nature teaches us that change is an intrinsic part of life and that we should find this a benefit, rather than something to be afraid of or to be resisted. Learning to embrace change can be a really positive influence and can leave us open to new ideas and more sustainable ways of living. Every full moon should be a subtle reminder that everything comes full circle and that change is something to be endorsed. In times of rapid societal change, spending time in nature allows us to observe that change is part and parcel of everyday life, but by taking a slower and more considered route similar to natural rhythms, we can explore how to adapt and find comfort in the cycles of growth and decay.

Today's gardeners have the amazing opportunity to choose plants which originate from all around the world. Back in the old days, gardeners had a rather more limited palette of plants to paint with; it was more likely that they were at least familiar with the wild plants they chose to offer garden space to. Many people are unaware of the global origins of their plants, so a little time to investigate the geographical roots of a plant can pay dividends. The origins of a plant in the wild can tell you a lot about its preferred conditions. Species which are found in woodlands are going to want some shade and shelter with a nice humus-rich soil, whereas species that are frequently found on the tops of mountains require bright sunshine and good drainage. Mixing up these plants and their needs is going to lead to frustrated gardeners and unhealthy specimens. Once you have learnt a little about their heritage and origins, the next thing to consider is their personalities or strategies for survival.

Plant strategies are the ways in which a plant attempts to make sure that its species succeeds. This can vary from being a short-growing, fast-maturing plant which puts its effort into creating lots of seed to spread around widely to build its population. The opposite of this is to grow slowly and to exist for a very long time, such as a tree. Different environments favour different strategies, although this is a changeable and dynamic situation and not one which remains static over time.

Ruderals, the colonisers

The first plant personality type or strategy that I want to discuss is the ruderal. The meaning of this word, according to the dictionary, is a plant which grows on waste ground or among rubbish – the word comes from the Latin word for rubble. A ruderal plant is an early coloniser of disturbed ground and bare soil. The disturbance may be caused by different factors in nature, such as fire, soil erosion or the activities of other species, such as herbivores or humans. These are frequently annual plants, although not always. They have the tendency to grow quickly, produce lots of seed, and therefore seedlings, and are often short lived. As humans are the species most likely to have created the disturbance, through agriculture, development or just removal of the plant species which were growing there previously, these plants are often the ones we call weeds. These are the early arrivals to the party. They can be useful to create a feeling of something happening by ensuring that the soil is not left entirely bare and creating the conditions to encourage a more diverse mix of plants to grow in that location. In party terms, these are the ones who forge the atmosphere going forwards, forming a buzz of excitement and creating the conditions for more botanical experimentation. Such plants include corn poppies, groundsel, dandelions and nettles. They often have high nutrient requirements and do not tolerate competition from other plants very well. Interestingly, many of our most common food crops are developed from ruderal species from other parts of the world, such as wheat and barley, as well as most of our vegetables.

Stress tolerators – the survivors

The second type of plants are called the stress tolerators. These plants have adapted to grow in environments which are limiting and don't offer perfect growing conditions. These more challenging ecosystems tend to severely limit the growth capabilities of many plant types, as well as their ability to spread. Stress factors include such things as very low or even high temperatures, or a shortage of water, light or nutrients. These plants have learnt to survive by choosing such places which are frequently isolated from other habitats, thus reducing competition. Stress tolerant plants have also evolved various coping mechanisms and characteristics that enable them to survive despite the inhospitable conditions, such as having hairy leaves to reduce water loss in dry areas or else strongly scented foliage, which can be a deterrent to any grazing animals considering eating them. Woodland plants fall into this category, particularly in deciduous woods, where not only do they have to compete for water and nutrients at ground level with the established root systems of large trees but their window for good light levels is brief and many of them have to emerge, flower and set seed before the appearance of the dense, leafy canopy of trees. They tend to be summer dormant, where they simply die back and bide their time until their own leaves are able to photosynthesise.

Stress tolerators are adaptable, thrifty and are often slow growing, becoming well suited to their individual habitats. They are content to share their space with others, as long as the relationship is relatively equal and no one species has the upper hand. However, if you put them in a garden setting where the environmental conditions are more suitable and are without the limiting factor on growth, they are able to grow much more easily. Usually, they are unable to co-exist with plant species which have much better strategies for growing under these conditions and can be crowded out by faster-growing plants and tend to be overwhelmed by them.

Some of my favourite plants fall into the category of being stress tolerators, particularly woodland plants which require deep damp soils and dappled shade. I also class plants such as peonies, many of the alpine or rockery plants and also lots of wild flowers in this category. Some highly domesticated plants also seem to act in the same way. Plants such as *Delphiniums,* while they require perfect growing conditions, also don't like to share their space with other plants as they are unable to compete with them. It was while explaining this to a friend one day, that she suddenly realised that this was where she had been going wrong and she understood that they simply need their space, just like some people do. She still refers to having 'Delphinium Days' for when she can't be doing with the interactions of other people and prefers to spend time alone.

Competitors – the bold and bossy ones

The third and final strategy or personality type of plants are the competitors. Their routes to success are almost self-explanatory, although we more often expect to see this sort of behaviour in animals rather than plants. These plants, rather like people are those who are bold and brassy, thrive in easy growing conditions and succeed by crowding out any plant types who aren't as strong growing as themselves They succeed by being the best, by growing fast and by being the first to take advantage of available resources within an area. They compete for water, nutrients and light and therefore tend to grow tall, in order to access the best light levels and are deep rooted in order to reach sufficient water and nutrients in the soil. There are a very wide number and variety of plants who use competition as their main strategy, from small herbaceous plants through to trees. Competitors will usually succeed in crowding out both the ruderals and the stress tolerators and, as such, these groups are best not mixed up in the border. Rather like the loud-mouthed bore at a dinner party, who drowns out the voices of the quieter, timid guests (who may well be really interesting) and eventually makes them give up and go home early, plant competitors are noted for their thuggish tendencies in crowding out others. Such plants include many of the Michaelmas daisy or Aster varieties, some types of *Rudbeckia* or cone flower, *Alchemilla mollis* or lady's mantle and the Japanese anemones. There are of course many more, as you will learn in your observations of plants in the garden. Indeed, some plants are absolute monsters in some situations but not others and this varies from place to place, often dependent on soil types or microclimate. A good example of this is when plants are introduced from other countries for their garden worthiness, but when they escape the garden confines, they become pests in the wild. Plants such as Japanese knotweed and Himalayan balsam are two such nuisances here in the UK.

Not all competitors are thugs, however, as trees also use this strategy to succeed. They combine their competitive habits with a foolproof technique of being extremely long lived and by putting all of their resources into creating huge woody structures which are long lasting and resilient. They are competitive in that they tend to be the tallest plants in an environment and their roots systems are large, frequently exceeding the extent of their leafy canopies.

Some trees even make further efforts to deter other plants from growing near them by producing chemicals at their roots which act as a means of stopping germination of any other species. This technique is known as allelopathy and trees such as walnuts and magnolias are extremely adept at using this strategy to claim a patch of land as their own. Allelopathic chemicals are able to inhibit growth and development of other plants and I believe that there are scientists looking into this behaviour of trees in the hope that they can isolate the chemical concerned in order to produce a more natural form of weed killer. Given that trees are in it for the long term, this seems like a very effective strategy for ensuring that they are able to exploit the maximum resources from the habitat, especially since they are unable to relocate themselves.

Placing plants into just a few categories can be considered over simplistic in many ways and is only intended as a guide to designing with plants. For the same reasons that it isn't always helpful to lump people in generalised groups like extrovert or introvert, optimist or pessimist, it only has a limited use in real life. Just like people, plant personalities can be complex and nuanced, often combining the characteristics of more than one aspect. Competitive ruderals are a classification in themselves, but it's all too easy to get bogged down in trying to pigeonhole everything, when in reality we simply need to trust our own observations. It's rather like trying to be a good party host – making sure that everyone has everything they need, that individuals are getting along well and that no one is left sitting in a corner on their own without a drink.

Clearly, plants are unable to move around very easily of their own accord in the wild. It has even been suggested that plants might have evolved to produce attractive flowers and delicious sweet fruit, which are attractive to humans, in an effort to encourage us to spread these plants around far more effectively than they would be able to without our help. Whether this is true or not, if this actually was their aim I would suggest that they have been incredibly successful. The fact that we have entire industries dedicated to the propagation and distribution of plant species is quite a feat!

Nurseries and garden centres appeal to our visual senses and frequently stock plants when they are flowering. We can see the beauty that they offer and we are often seduced into buying them despite not really knowing what sort of conditions they like to grow in. This appeals to the magpie side of us and is a trick that we are all liable to succumb to, so don't be too hard on yourself if you have fallen for it. When I have bought something entirely unsuitable for my garden, I keep plants in pots. These get moved around until I either find a place where they appear to want to grow, or else they spend their entire lives in pots, usually outside the back door, as a reminder to me to stop being so impulsive when I see a bargain.

Learning to understand more about plants and their tricks of the trade can make for incredible insights. There have been a few notable plantspeople who have used this knowledge to their advantage. A particularly outstanding example is Luther Burbank, who was a pioneering American plant breeder at the turn of the last century. Burbank was responsible for over 800 new varieties of plants during his career, including the Burbank potato, still widely used. He was affectionately known as the 'Plant Wizard' due to his highly unorthodox methods. Often criticised for his lack of scientific technique, Burbank claimed to be able to talk with his plants and ask them to work with him when he had a particular outcome in mind. Whether this is believable or not, his careful observation of plant characteristics is evident in his hybridisation and breeding of plant varieties. From spineless cacti to giant cherries, his results were outstanding and incredibly prolific, with an estimated three new plants varieties created every week of his working life. The Shasta daisy was one of his most popular creations and is still commonly grown today.

You will begin to understand plant communities more easily if you think of how long they might have been established. Immature communities and ecosystems are characterised by head-long growth and competition. These situations are typical of new gardens and these often require a higher degree of intervention in the early days, rather akin to bringing up young people or animals. On the opposite end of the spectrum, a mature ecosystem works more by co-operation, interdependency and the sharing and recycling of resources. This would be our ideal garden situation if very low-maintenance levels are your aim. In real life, we tend to find that we end up with some areas of mature ecosystem and some of the more dynamic, changing and immature systems, especially if we enjoy growing vegetables or annual flowers.

Grouping plants which have similar characteristics of growth generally means that they will grow well together. Planting a bunch of thugs together might mean that some are more aggressive growers than others but, as a rule of thumb, they should be able to co-exist in some form and this type of planting is a really useful way of crowding out the weed plants that you don't want. Planting a competitor in with the stress tolerators will usually end in either the competitor taking over completely (unless you are prepared to keep it under control) or else the competitor will sulk if conditions aren't ideal and will not thrive. Sick plants attract pests and diseases, so it is always best to ensure your plants are healthy. Generally, the ruderals, particularly the annuals, will continue to require you to sow seed and work the soil in order for them to return every year, just as we have to in the vegetable plot. This requires time and effort, and although I am happy to do this for the food I eat, I am much less inclined to do this in the ornamental garden. Due to needing to keep some areas clear for growing vegetables from seed, I usually save myself the effort and grow any annual flowers in these same spaces. That way I am only having to cultivate a few areas of soil, plus planting flowers alongside vegetables encourages pollinators and predators of common pests.

As always, aim to ensure that there is as little bare soil exposed as possible in the main growing season. In spring, you can cover the soil by planting bulbs, which will die back to make room for the summer's more luxuriant growth. This is the fun and creative side of gardening. Following the basic rule of plant personalities and preferences will ensure that your choices will thrive, allowing you the chance to paint pictures in flowers and foliage.

Thinking about things from a plant's perspective also puts you in a position of allowing nature to create a useful and mutually agreeable community, with just a gentle helping hand from the gardener. Planning is useful, as is learning about the plants we want to have in our garden. If we can avoid the mistakes from the beginning, by taking time to understand plants and their needs, we can then allow things to develop naturally while we enjoy ourselves in the garden we have helped to create. Often the smallest of interventions or even non-interventions can, over time, make a big difference to a habitat. Our job here is to understand when we need to become involved in the process and when we should just sit back and watch what happens. This is of course the exact opposite of the television garden make-over programmes which were so popular back in the day. I often wonder how many of those gardens look now. While this approach is very unlikely to make good television, I can assure you that your garden will be much more successful and long lived, without too much work from you.

The end of August brings the winds of change, as autumn sends envoys ahead on north-westerlies. Sharp heavy showers, so much longed-for only a few weeks earlier, now appear scolding and dour. The vitality of the growing season reaches its glorious climax with a culmination of colour. A vibrant selection of floral treats offer themselves for my appreciation, like a motley pick and mix counter of sweet delights. Azure Asters, cardinal Crocosmia and amber tufts of golden rod make their appearance in the long wild border, uncivilised competitors all holding their own in a battle of flowery dominion and awash with a feeding frenzy of flying insects. The grasses thrust their flowerheads upwards, high above their foliage, swaying wildly in the slightest of breezes, fountains of fine inflorescences. Toadstools appear daily in the woodland, the work of the Fae folk. Mysterious in their habits, their coloured caps varying wildly in colour, size and shape.

After a month of near silence, the mornings are once again marked by the song of the robin, honing his vocal talent in readiness for the following year. The nights begin to arrive early like over enthusiastic party goers, awkward at first but quickly making themselves at home. We light the woodburning stove in the kitchen to keep the evening chill at bay and begin the season of slow-cooked stews as a welcome by-product. The scent of woodsmoke hangs in the air, joining the scent of damp earth and still warm stone walls. Late summer's mutable moods are echoed in the landscape, hazy low-lying mists adding extra layers of interest and depth to the views over the hills in the distance.

This is the time of harvesting. My days are spent chopping and preparing fruits and vegetables for preserving. The kitchen is a whirl of jam and chutney making and the freezer becomes ever fuller with roasted and stewed tomatoes, and bags of runner beans. The pumpkins are carefully severed from their vines and gently set to ripen in the greenhouse before bringing them into the house for storage and decoration. As tedious as this work becomes, I know that I will be appreciative of these summer treats once the winter arrives, and that nothing comes close to home-grown vegetables, despite the fact that all of these things can be flown in to supermarkets from far-flung places. I am reminded of my grandmother whose pantry shelves were always full of bottled produce, in the days before freezers and dehydrators made our lives easier. This simple act of preserving the harvest is a timeless one; it has been the focus of generations of women before me. I am grateful to be carrying on an age-old tradition and, more than that, I am profoundly aware that the nutrition I am storing will help to keep me healthy, well and active through the colder months ahead.

Invitations to celebrate the season

- Put your houseplants outside when it rains. This is a great way to refresh your plants by giving them a good soak and letting the rain wash the dust from their leaves. Don't leave them out in full sun if they're not used to it, as this can cause their leaves to scorch.

- Go for a walk and see if there are any blackberries ripening yet. Blackberries are a superfood, just as nutritious as blueberries, and just as tasty, but free for the picking. I give them a quick rinse once I'm home, then I freeze them on a tray, before storing them in bags for use through the winter months. Blackberries also make great jams and jellies, or cordials, which preserves their goodness and can make great gifts to give away.

- Consider not deadheading your flowers once they have finished blooming. The seed heads which will then appear can offer a great food source for seed-eating birds such as greenfinch and goldfinch later in the year. Plus, you get to enjoy the sculptural shapes of the seed heads through the winter months. Many of them look amazing with a light coating of frost or snow. Even roses can be left to form hips towards the end of the year, another valuable food for thrushes and blackbirds and a source of much-needed colour in the winter garden.

- Build a little log pile next to your pond, or in a shady out of the way corner of the garden. This is the time of year when creatures are beginning to scout out suitable hibernation places for when the weather turns colder. Can you incorporate a hedgehog home too?

- Enjoy the smell of autumn when you are outside. Breathe in the earthy scent of fallen foliage. One of my favourite trees is the katsura, which comes from Japan, and it emits the smell of candy floss or burnt sugar as its leaves turn yellow.

- Consider saving seed from your favourite plants, so you can grow more or share with friends and family. Collect seedheads on dry days and keep in a paper bag, in a cool dry place.

CHAPTER TEN

Mabon: The Autumn Equinox

A gentle early autumn day, with a gentle warm breeze, white clouds and sunshine. I celebrate the equinox by making a circular leaf and seed head mandala on the lawn, from the various leaves of trees and shrubs which were starting the early transition to autumn colours. Metallic hues and shades emerge in the garden now – copper, bronze, gold and rust. The trees' own version of alchemy at play as precious metals are created from sunlight, cool temperatures and rain. I realise suddenly that the swallows have left. They had been lining up on the wires for a few days now, chattering their excitement as their long journey to warmer climes approached. I'm sad that I didn't get the chance to say goodbye and I will miss them. The moon is waning, a bright slender sickle hanging low in the evening sky as I walk the dogs. The year is waning too, shorter days, the sun, bright as it is, yields only a comfortable warmth. A far cry from the intense heat of only a few weeks earlier.

I toss a few wildflower seed bombs under the hedge bottoms; now that they are beginning to create a screen, I want them to look as natural as possible, so introducing a few different wild species should help. Planting wild flowers at this time of year is, in my experience, the best time. Some will germinate early and over winter as tiny plants. Others will bide their time, as they need the cold to break their dormancy, and will only deign to appear next spring. I wish them well as I plant. It's bulb-planting time too and my shed is full of boxes of many different varieties, tulips, daffodils, snakeshead fritillaries, lilies, crocus and many more. Most of them are for my design customers but, as ever, while ordering for other people, there are always a few which fall into my virtual basket, despite saying every year that I have enough spring bulbs in the garden. I always think that planting bulbs is probably the nearest I get to instant gardening, as in a few short months, they will emerge and make a wonderful splash of colour without the need to wait years, or spend a great deal of money in planting mature trees or shrubs.

Autumn teaches us to slow down in anticipation of winter and encourages us to appreciate the less hurried pace of life once the peak of growing activity comes to an end. More time to reflect on the year that has been and celebrate our successes and note those things that we could maybe have done differently. The beginning of the end of the growing cycle is heralded by fabulous autumn colours, these showing themselves to us only by the process of plants stopping photosynthesis in preparation for dormancy in the depths of winter. These glorious shades were there all along but were masked by the bright green colour of chlorophyll which is part of the alchemy which enables plants to gain energy from sunlight. Suddenly, when the temperatures start to drop and the days become shorter after the autumnal equinox, these colours are revealed to us in all their magnificence. A brief but show-stopping display, almost better than the floral highlights of midsummer. What do we hide from the world by masking our beautiful shades with the bright green hues of overwork and staying constantly busy? Perhaps it might be possible now to see these multicoloured layers of what lies beneath, that only become visible to us when we stop chasing work and slow down. Appreciate the beauty of the autumn and take it as a reminder that as human beings we weren't designed to fill our lives with productivity every day, all year round. Perhaps a little more time to sit and think, plot and plan, remember and reminisce is just as essential to growth as being busy all the time.

Leaving the leaves in place enables the decay which is the building block for new growth next year to take place exactly where it is needed. After this we get to see the bones of the garden, skeletal in its architectural beauty, stark contrasts against pale winter skies. As nature strips away the flounce and showiness of leaves and flowers, we get to see what lies behind. Like ourselves, a garden needs a strong structure to support it; without this framework on which to hang the fruits, flowers and foliage, the effect is chaotic and liable to damage from outside agents. Structure can be seen as the opposite of creativity in life, but I prefer to see it as the essential sturdiness we need in order to branch out and extend ourselves. It is only in winter that we can see the wood from the trees; only when we're not distracted by all that is bright and beautiful, can we see whether there is sufficient strength on which to build our summer growth.

Saving seeds

The adventure of growing from seed is a natural process which we can all play a part in; however, when we need to buy in our seed every year, we are still dependent upon large companies to supply our needs. One way of completing the cycle of growth independently is to consider saving seeds for ourselves. This is a relatively simple procedure for many plants, although there are some which require a little more thought and planning.

Most of our commercial seed is now in the hands of a very few global companies. Where there used to be plenty of smaller seed companies, serving local markets and customers, these have been taken over by the larger companies, a familiar pattern typical of the current economic system we find ourselves in. When so few businesses have the market for seed, this makes growers vulnerable to price hikes, lack of variety and the loss of heritage and heirloom species. Therefore, the knowledge to save seed as our forebears did may be the only way to keep some of the older varieties going, ensuring diversity and generally making us less reliant on mega-corporations who don't always have our best interests at heart.

As I have previously mentioned, the growth of F1 hybrids in the seed market means that these plants are not able to be saved from seed, since as hybrids they are unlikely to reproduce properly. I have occasionally saved seed from hybrids and although a few plants shared the characteristics of their parent plant, these were few and I ended up with a range of plants which didn't really provide what I needed.

F1 hybrids usually have a short lifespan, as the methods used for their production mean that they are produced from a very limited gene pool, which over time leads to weaker and less resilient plants, therefore new hybrid varieties are consistently required. F1 hybrids are also bred to be grown with the variety of artificial inputs available to large-scale growers, which can mean that the organic home grower is at a distinct disadvantage.

Growing and saving seed which has been 'open pollinated' allows for more diversity. Open pollination means that we rely on natural methods to pollinate the flowers; the work is often done by pollinating insects of all types, although of course bees are the most recognised for their endeavours in this aspect. We gardeners are also able to influence this pollination if we choose, as we too recognise that we are part of nature. The genetic material present within these plants is available for anyone to use and is not controlled by companies or organisations. It is hands-down the best option for organic growers and as garden alchemists, this should be precisely the type of experimentation we are engaged in.

Therefore, open-pollinated plants are what we need to grow in order to be able to save seed from them. Many of the older varieties work this way and for many years over countless generations, this is probably how they were kept from year to year. The biggest advantage of saving your own seed, especially if you choose the biggest and best plants to save your seed from, is that, over time, the plants become better adapted to your own growing environment, soils and weather patterns. You can select for bigger flowers, better-tasting vegetables, smaller and more prolific fruits, unusual coloured leaves, or indeed any particular trait that you wish to encourage. The ability of plants to adapt to local conditions means that you will end up with a more robust and better-suited range of plants, which are potentially able to withstand pests and diseases more effectively.

Hybridisation is, of course, something which can also happen naturally and doesn't need to take place under the watchful eye of humans. In the case of vegetables, this can sometimes mean that we end up with crops which aren't edible, such as when an edible squash cross-pollinates with an ornamental variety, causing the fruits to be bitter and unpleasant tasting at best and potentially poisonous as a worst-case scenario. The home seed saver needs to be aware of this danger and anyone wishing to save vegetable seeds should make sure that they learn which of their crops are liable to cross-pollinate and take steps to ensure that this doesn't happen. In the case of flowers, unless you are planning to eat them, this is much less of a risk. The main dangers when saving seed from ornamental plants is that you might inadvertently fall foul of the legal restrictions of Plant Breeders Rights, which is a way for commercial nurseries to patent the intellectual rights to new varieties of plants. Many of the new plants which are launched at the flower shows such as Chelsea are liable to have PBR restrictions on them, making it illegal for anyone to propagate those plants by any means, whether by seed or cuttings.

Seed saving is as simple as allowing plants to flower and then set seed. That's it really, a natural state of affairs which has been going on since plants first appeared on earth. After that, it is just a matter of harvesting the seed once it is ripe and before the plant drops the seed or the birds get to it first. I pick seed heads and store them in paper bags in a cool dry place until I have time to separate them properly from their seed cases. In some parts of my garden I allow things to self-seed, which basically means that the seed drops to the earth of its own accord and then it is allowed to germinate when the time is right. This provides me with a surprise display every year, as I never know exactly whereabouts flowers will pop up. I love this random and slightly chaotic state of affairs as it sometimes rewards you with some stunning planting combinations and you can always pull up any seedlings which are in the wrong place and either compost them or pot them up and give them to friends and neighbours. I even do this with vegetables and I have discovered that parsnip, which has always been a tricky plant to germinate, now is one of my most productive vegetables. The only down side being that it refuses to grow in rows!

Everything in the garden is lovely, as we approach the end of September. I refuse to cut back and deadhead the wild borders. There are times when it makes the overall effect a little unkempt, but I am learning to love the chaotic appearance. The brown stems, dying leaves and seed heads signal the progression of the year and I am happy that this is the way of things at this time. Beneath the old crab apple, the lawn is adorned with golden speckled leaves, cast off early along with the first of the scarlet-toned windfall fruits. I think it is a perfect vignette of the contrast of natural abundance and the shedding of things no longer required and I note that I might take some of my teetering pile of read books to the charity shop, in celebration of the season.

These things which some find untidy in their ordered and pristine environment bring me joy with their habit of injecting a sense of spontaneity into the proceedings. I admire the effect of a fallen leaf in contrast to a neatly clipped lawn or the appearance of russet polka dots on a previously uniform green leaf. Hogweed stems, once the bearers of plates of creamy-white petals, turn slowly as they age to rusty candelabras, their seeds held aloft as offerings to blunt-billed birds.

Permaculture Principle: Catch and store energy

This principle starts from the understanding that energy is an abundant resource and that we need to know how to make the best use of it. From rainwater catchment, making the most use of a sheltered microclimate, growing our own food and using renewable energy, this principle teaches us to see how we can reduce our footprint on the earth and wisely use the resources we have available. We have all, of course, been led astray somewhat by our use of fossil fuels, which, although initially abundant, have become problematic by our unlimited use of them. However, as prices of such energy become ever more expensive and their use has caused our global climate to be increasingly unstable, we need to learn to be more resourceful in alternative forms of energy which are less damaging and available to all. I like to think that the winter squash and pumpkins, which I harvest from the garden and store on a cool shelf in the pantry, are a form of captured winter sunshine which fills me with energy through the winter months, when we slice them into fat wedges and drizzle with oil before we bake them in the wood stove and eat them with spicy lentil dal or leek risotto.

Working to catch and store energy is a particularly poignant lesson for me, as learning to work with the ebbs and flows of my own personal energy levels has been one of the most difficult aspects of learning to live with a chronic illness. Allowing myself to do less through the winter months at a time when nature is mostly dormant has helped me to make the most of my time and energy and prepare myself for the busy period when spring arrives. Capturing energy on a personal level is related directly to what I choose to eat. I found that by paying more attention to my diet and eating more fruit and vegetables and a lot less in the way of processed food made a huge difference to how I felt. While it does take more effort to cook from scratch, source organic products and eat seasonally, I have found that it is worth the extra work and my health is improving dramatically as a result.

Natural gardening

Natural gardening embraces a completely different mentality, one which doesn't view nature as something to be controlled or tamed but something that we are elementally part of. A look at the methods used by ancient and indigenous people who lived on the land, growing crops and harvesting wild food, shows that their understanding of how to work with the earth was deep rooted and distinctive to the places and communities where they lived. They had an inherent knowledge of their native lands, learnt over many generations and passed down by teachings, which emphasised the importance of the land and its gifts to humankind. They learnt to take only as much as they needed, to leave some for others and to be grateful for what they harvested. In modern society, we seem to have forgotten much of this old knowledge. We now rely on science to provide our narrative about how nature works. We consider ourselves superior to other life forms and assume we are now able to bypass the limits first determined by our working within the natural planetary systems. It seems to be a problem of both imagination and understanding.

Natural gardening is tricky to define and wild gardening doesn't really fare any better. The words wild and natural have become rather negative in their connotations, especially in regards to the garden. A garden, as we have discovered, is where human intervention is evident and nature has been tamed, cultivated and controlled – almost out of existence. Wildness is thought to be an untended and overgrown wasteland, the opposite of what a garden should be. So, is natural gardening an oxymoron? Do the two terms cancel each other out, leading to confusion as to who is in charge – man or nature? Now that we are facing a crisis with wildlife numbers declining rapidly and the impacts of climate change knocking on our door, we must redefine the garden. Could we re-imagine our gardens as providing us with all we need, while also addressing these issues and doing something positive to improve the situation? We can, if we are careful and considered in our actions, make this benefit ourselves as well as the wider ecosystems we inhabit and depend on. We even can use this impetus to tackle our own nature deficit disorder.

The happy gardening life

Ask almost anyone what they want from life and the answer is often that they want to be happy. Initially, people might suggest wealth, expensive objects, comfort or meaningful relationships, but investigate more thoroughly and it is mainly happiness and peacefulness we all seek. Studies have shown that today's lifestyles aren't really designed around the pursuit of happiness … instead we are bombarded with advertising telling us that we're not good enough as we are and that we need to buy a bewildering array of products in order to bring us happiness. However, if this was true, then the market for such products would surely have dried up by now. Shopping and retail therapy are clearly not the answer, but we are caught on a treadmill of work and consumption, where even our leisure pursuits urge us to keep busy or buy the latest gadget to fill the hours when we're not working. We have been trained to think that doing nothing is boring and a waste of our precious and limited time.

Our brains have evolved over thousands of years to keep us forever alert to perceived dangers. In modern times, with fewer physical dangers than in our hunter gatherer past, this constant state of alertness can make us anxious and unsettled. The constant chatter of the internal voice haunts our waking hours, confirming our suspicions that we're not good enough, or we worry about what the future holds and we mull over past events and berate ourselves for our mistakes. Humans are very good at being unhappy. In fact, our brains are wired to make it easier to remember the things that went wrong rather than things which went well. Originally, this helped us avoid repeating life-threatening actions, but it also makes us focus on the negative aspects of life, which over time makes us sad and anxious.

There are, however, ancient traditions in many religions which suggest that contemplation or meditation can help us achieve a happier and more peaceful frame of mind, no matter what our circumstances. In recent times, these traditions have been reframed as mindfulness, a secular, non-religious approach to practising the calming and focusing of the mind. One of the first advocates of mindfulness, an American professor Jon Kabat Zinn, describes it as 'paying attention, on purpose, in the present moment, non-judgmentally'. This can be as simple as sitting and breathing, giving your attention to that alone and trying not to let your mind wander off on some random journey or narrative. This is easier said than done and it can take a while to train the brain to do as you wish. In fact, I have known cocker spaniel puppies with better recall than my own brain, so I personally prefer to pay attention in the garden.

I wake up feeling stressed and tired. I have been working hard recently and there is still so much to do in the garden, that it feels like yet another chore. I chide myself gently and remind myself that nature allows us to make mistakes, take our time over things, and the fact that I haven't cleared the polytunnel ready to plant winter vegetables doesn't really matter too much and that it will wait until the weekend. I go outside with my cup of tea and take five minutes to see if I can find a moment of calm, to try and start the day in a better frame of mind. It's a chilly October morning and the wind ruffles my hair, making me shiver. I feel like autumn is nipping at summer's heels, chivvying her along as she graciously descends the grand staircase to take her final bow before leaving the stage. The leaves are changing, a subtle fade to a more colourful palette and a reminder that change is coming. The sun appears over the tops of the trees and I realise that it's going to be a beautiful morning. Already I feel in a more positive frame of mind and I smile, thankful for the gentle nudge to make the most of the good days, to soak up the heat and light before they dwindle.

Making your garden a place of sanctuary for yourself should always be part of your plan. Placing a bench or chair in a quiet corner, preferably where you have a feeling of privacy, surrounded by leafy shrubs or flowers, maybe where you can watch the birds on a feeder, or close to a water feature, where you can watch the rippling reflections of sunlight, is best. If possible, find a view, where you're not too distracted by your neighbours washing the car or the fact that you haven't put the bins out yet. Make it a place for your favourite flowers, where you can appreciate their colours and scents in closer detail. When I am out for a walk, I have a habit of picking up stones; unusual shapes or bright colours draw my eye to them and they get slipped into my jacket pocket. I then use them for putting around the tops of pots and planters, like a mulch, or I make small patterns with them on the surface of the soil as part of the flower bed. These stones each have a small story to tell, many of them remind me of walks on the beach or similarly I have bits of broken pottery from other people's gardens that I have worked in. They all bring back happy memories, which I am reminded of when I choose to be. I also collect unusual bits of wood, birds' feathers and pine cones and add them to my garden as a form of decoration. I guess it's me as an adult continuing the theme of having a nature table, like we had at primary school when I was very young, or else the fact that maybe I was a magpie in a previous life …

When my mother was very ill, I visited her most days in her care home on my way home from work. I would take her a little treasure from my day, a small bunch of flowering grasses, a larch twig with some cones on it, or a selection of leaves of different colours and sizes. We would sit together and look carefully at them and talk about the things from nature that I had brought her on that day. I think it helped us both, having these small wild gifts to talk about, to touch, smell and admire. She had fairly advanced dementia and it was too difficult to have meaningful conversations with her, but as she had been a keen gardener in her earlier life, the pleasure she got from exploring these simple items with me was very precious. By the time she died, she had a shelf full of natural beauty around her. I still have a couple of these things that I took to her in her last days and they continue to have the ability to bring back memories of that special time we had together near the end of her life.

Allowing nature to guide the way we garden can be very freeing. We spend a lot of our lives trying to control things and being sad or angry when we feel we can't, so sometimes letting go and seeing what happens can be a very insightful and surprisingly calming thing to do. Gardening is a frustrating game at times; while we can plan all we like, there will always be something to throw a spanner in the works. A late frost, too much or too little rain, or an invasion of caterpillars can all negatively affect our plans. However, not getting around to weeding out those tiny seedlings which appeared in your new border might mean you suddenly realise you have an abundance of foxglove seedlings to move around and share. Letting your grass grow long, instead of cutting it short every week might surprise you with some unexpected wild flowers popping up or an increase in the numbers of butterflies visiting. Noticing the changes in the same place day after day allows you to tune into and follow a different beat. Merely sitting or working at a simple task in your garden enables you to do just that and can change both how you garden and how you approach life in the wider sense.

Elderberries

The entrance path to the cottage is guarded by a rowan tree and an elder. These two native trees have long been associated with protection from evil spirits and have been planted as guardian trees at boundaries and by dwellings for many centuries. While this is clearly a practice which is dying out, it was at one time very common to see them by the entrances to older houses. Another way to protect a house included the burying of old shoes at the threshold to a dwelling. When we were digging out the earth floors of our cottage, to lay a damp-proof membrane and insulation, we discovered that an old knitted stocking had been buried by the doorway, presumably as a similar token. I can only suspect, in this particular case, that shoes were too precious a commodity to be buried under the floor of such a humble home.

I love elder bushes as they are fast growing, rather beautiful and have so many uses. There is an enormous specimen at the edge of the woods, the largest I have ever seen, a grandmother of trees if ever there was one. Their flowers make excellent summer cordials and tasty additions to gooseberry jam, while their berries are useful in making rather fine wines, jams, chutneys and my favourite winter drink of spiced elderberry cordial, which is a superb hot drink on a cold winter's day. It has the advantage of having anti-viral properties and lots of Vitamin C, so a perfect tonic to ward off colds and flu. This year I have found an old recipe for a sauce called Pontack, popular, apparently, in the seventeenth century as a seasoning, which relies on elderberries as its main ingredient. I decide to pick a basket of berries, as this year they are abundant and even though the birds have been gorging on them, there are still plenty left for me. Picking elderberries off their stalks is a labour of love, however, and soon my fingers are stained black with their juice. It takes four months for the sauce to mature and as I bottle it, I am reminded that the ability to wait for something to be at its best, is a lesson we are failing to learn these days. Patience was never my strong point, yet if we insisted on pulling up seedlings every day to see how well they were rooting, they would never grow. I put the bottle of sauce at the back of the cupboard and make a note in my diary to check it in the early spring.

Invitations to celebrate the season

- This is a great time to sow wild flowers. If you were inspired by leaving the grass to grow long back in May but were disappointed by the lack of flowers in your mini meadow, then now is the time to give nature a helping hand. Choose species which will do well in your soils and microclimate. Cut the grass as short as you are able and give the surface a stern raking over. This is a great job to do to release some pent-up stress or anger! This should expose some bare soil, creating suitable seedbeds for sowing the seed into. Trample it down a little after sowing and wait until spring to see what appears.

- Leave the leaves. If you find that your garden is full of leaves at this time of year, please see this as a cause for celebration, rather than a nuisance. If you need to rake up to keep hard landscaped areas or lawns clear, then pile the leaves on to your flower borders and let them rot down in situ. The worms will be delighted with your offerings of organic matter, the leaves will help protect the soil surface through the winter and your plants will grow a lot better next year.

- Harvest the last of any wild food, herbs or vegetables you have grown in the garden. Make herb vinegars, jams and pickles, either for yourself or to give as gifts.

- If you have been spending the longer evenings planning changes to your garden, and you are thinking about extending or making new beds and borders, this is a good time to mark them out. You can begin your no-dig beds at this time of year, by laying double thickness cardboard over the areas you wish to become planting areas. On top of this, spread compost, grass clippings, autumn leaves, woodchip or whatever you have to hand, to a depth of around 10 centimetres. This will rot down over the winter with the help of the soil organisms, making a rich layer of earth, ready to plant into next spring.

FULL CIRCLE

CHAPTER ELEVEN

Full Circle

The alchemy of gardening is a heartfelt plea for the return of wildness, nature and joyous experimentation into our lives. We have explored the history of gardens and charted the progress through time of our relationship with nature and the natural world. Having picked apart the threads of gardening techniques and philosophies, we have questioned where we might have made errors and if we are able to make amends. Our deep need for nature connection and our reliance on the web of life points us towards a more holistic approach to managing our gardens and outdoor spaces. A successful garden is a misnomer because there will always be things which could be improved. In a variety of ways, we need to learn to accept our failures and learn from the experience in the hope that we will be better next year. Gardening teaches us hope and patience. A garden is only ever on loan to us and we are simply its temporary custodians. We shouldn't treat it as a financial investment or a showcase for the latest and greatest in horticulture. A garden is a small patch of land that we have the privilege of getting to know well, one which encourages us to put down roots into fertile soil, and this brings with it the responsibility to care for the land in a careful and considered way. If we can do this with an eye to its representation as a fragment of a much wider environment, then we should be able to ensure that we leave it in a better state than we found it.

It goes without question now, that human activity has damaged the fragile ecosystems on which our planet depends. For decades, we have overspent on our accounts and plundered the reserves to leave a gaping empty hole. Our failure to address this excessive behaviour is leading to the situation where not only nature is at risk from pollution, climate change and disease but our own lives and livelihoods too. That this world does not belong solely to us, is at the heart of this discussion and it is past the time when we need to focus on positive solutions rather than burying our heads in the sand and attempting to conduct business as usual. The problems began when we started to think about nature as something separate, something we were able to manage and control. We distanced ourselves physically, emotionally and intellectually from nature. When we talk about nature, we refer to it as an abstraction, an external entity which exists only outside of ourselves. The truth we now must accept is that nature is a complex collection of fascinating beings which are involved in an intricate inter-weaving dance of co-dependency, of which we are part and parcel.

As a society, we have become indifferent and even hostile towards the nature which exists on our doorsteps. Nature has instead, become a destination, a leisure pursuit, something to which we travel to admire from a distance. Instead, could we imagine allowing the wild edges to creep in a little closer into our safe and ordered lives? Those liminal spaces, the margins and corridors of living things could become a lifeline. We can make a home for nature right outside our doors, if we choose to. In order to work with nature, we must match our actions to these rhythms and cycles and learn to appreciate the work which is done for us by the systems and their associated organisms already in place. We cannot do this if we are unaware of their existence, so we need to learn to recognise them as allies and kin.

In the face of such seemingly huge and intractable issues, the suggestion that gardening can be part of the solution might seem simplistic, even risible. However, by acting responsibly within our own small sphere of influence, we can not only make a difference but perhaps, more importantly, change our minds about how we perceive our own identities within the interactions of the wild world. Although these simple actions towards changing our own intimate, domestic environments might at first seem insignificant, the effects taken as a whole could in reality be groundbreaking. By altering the ways in which we regard our own gardens and the open spaces in our communities, and by managing them with a lighter touch, we can begin to heal some of the damage we have wrought on the earth. In doing so, we can also rediscover that a deeper connection to nature could enrich our day-to-day existence far more than we could imagine.

We learn these things by simple actions of observing and doing. By making slow, considered and informed interventions, we can discover in a more open-minded and less-controlling way to garden. This enables us to find more enjoyment in our hands-on gardening experiences, which involve less physical work and offer us more time with which to appreciate the beauty and soothing effects of spending time in the nature on our doorsteps. In taking these ideas and implementing them in our own gardens, we can find the joy in having wildness close at hand. We can appreciate the unexpected, the overexuberant and the boisterousness of allowing plants to exhibit their natural tendencies. We can cultivate a passion for dandelions, marvel at the tenacity of nettles and even begin to tolerate the aphids on our rose bushes. As we learn to slow down and watch this great unfolding, we will notice the bumblebees which revel in the feast of pollen and nectar offered up by the dandelions' generous flowers, wonder at the squirming mass of tortoiseshell caterpillars which can strip the leaves from nettles in a matter of days and cheer on the blue tits as they collect the insects from our plants to feed their growing broods. All of this bounty has its place and its part to play – and who are we to decide otherwise?

This alchemy can make us dreamers and believers in magic. The plants we choose to grow can echo the beauty of the wild we see around us and bring us the joy of the ever-changing progression through the year and the slow but certain growth of plants. To plant a tree is to have hope. Trees, slow growing by our own standards at least, are an investment of time which pays its dividends into the future. Planting hopefully, whether a seed or a tree, takes you away from your present situation and teaches you that some things take their own time in coming to fruition. Plants allow us to experience first-hand the seasonal shifts which occur throughout the year. In the native plants of the countryside, as well as the bewildering choices available to us as gardeners, we can enhance our appreciation of these cycles and rhythms. From the first glimpse of a snowdrop pushing up from the earth in January, through to the glorious colours of autumn in November, we can find solace and stability simply by pausing and enjoying these gifts from nature. Even the stillness and stark silhouettes of deep winter have their own particular charm.

It is up to us to creatively respond to the clues given to us as we learn to be still and observe carefully. Each garden is different and each area within that space offers new and interesting possibilities. Garden alchemy is based upon some scientific rules, some insightful philosophies and allowing nature to flourish freely, with only the lightest of touches from the gardener. You will need to attend to things carefully when exploring what is the most mutually supportive relationship you can nurture with the wild. Let us be curious and inquisitive about what nature might conjure up, if given the chance.

This is the art of slow gardening. Letting nature set the pace. Finding enjoyment by being present rather than by doing, the gentle cadence of growth and senescence flow to and fro like the tide. Despite our longing for progression and certainty, it soothes us, by teaching us to pay attention to the small things and finding enchantment in the ordinary. Discovering that nature is a steadying constant, a source of wonder and a reliable barometer of change and that you are a part of it all, is a balm to our fractured existence. Simply knowing that your considered and mindful stewardship of the land does make a difference is a vital step. By working together, we can achieve so much more than if we were forging two separate diverging paths. The essence of how gardening teaches us about time is that, no matter how hard we try, we never manage to 'get on top of' our lists of things to do. In fact, the faster we work at trying to fit everything in, the longer the list becomes. The answer is to stop and pause for a while. Or just do something simple, small and insignificant. It doesn't matter. Let the borders go unweeded or the roses unpruned. They'll cope. The paradox is that the more effort you spend in trying to get through the endless tasks, the less you will enjoy your time in the garden and – let's face it – what is the point in that?

Fashions change all the time, so let us become gardening trend setters. It is time for alchemy to begin to emerge from the shadows. I demand that messy and wild becomes the new neat and tidy. Let's celebrate spontaneity, unpredictability, the undomesticated and the feral. Why should our lives be conducted in ways which uproot us from our natural habitats and force us to live in places which are sterile, orderly and uninspiring with no place for wildness or connection to other living things. Can we allow the controlling grip of uniformity and monoculture to wither and die, so that in its place we can embrace a wild and dynamic aesthetic? A new movement where the weed-free lawn is seen as something weird and a sterile garden, devoid of life is nothing to aspire to. By all means, let's keep and preserve a few of these gardens and have them as museum pieces and places of education. We can visit them with our grandchildren and wonder at what made us think that such places were desirable or even practical. We can shake our heads at those gardeners who wasted all that time persecuting weeds, dowsing the earth with poisonous chemicals and trimming everything to within an inch of its life, rather than relaxing and enjoying the flowers, the birdsong and the butterflies. This might be our legacy, but not one we have to continue.

By harnessing the alchemy present within every garden, we might not be in the position of discovering the secret of immortality, although our gardens can teach us so much about life and death and the circle dance, they perform. We might not even learn to transmute base elements into gold, although we can discover wealth beyond our imagining. Alchemy is simply learning to harness the magic of nature and embrace the gifts that this can bring into our lives.

From the beginning, I have had no desire to be defined by my illness, yet it has and still does limit what I can do. Chronic illness never goes away. I have had to learn to incorporate it into my life and accept that it is an intrinsic part of myself. I have taken it as an invitation to listen and learn lessons from the more vulnerable and fragile aspects of being a human, those that we so frequently seem to neglect when we are in good health. I am, however, first and foremost a gardener. My illness has been a wake-up call and the positive aspect I can take from this episode of my life is that it has given me the opportunity to examine my gardening interventions more closely. It has forced me to slow down sufficiently to be able to observe and listen more attentively, as nature goes about her business. For many years, I thought that nature was my business, yet now I know that I am just one of the many beings which make up the workforce and the reality is that nature is a workers' co-operative. This has fundamentally changed my approach to gardening, it has opened up new ways of doing things and allowed me to stop doing those things which are unnecessary. I learnt that just as seeds need darkness in order to germinate, that I too needed to rest in a dark place for a while and recuperate in order to make a new start. It was in this dark place where I learnt my most profound lesson. That there is joy and beauty to be discovered in almost every moment, if we choose to look for it. We don't have to travel far or even look too hard to find it. By accepting the small and simple aspects of life as sparks for happiness, our lives will never be short of inspiration or meaning. All we have to do to achieve this is to pay attention to what is around us.

I have always considered that I am 'not very good at meditating', as my concentration is short of span and often tries to encompass too many things at once. I now know that gardening is my preferred method of being mindful and that the very actions involved in gardening are what keep bringing me back to the present, helping to stop my incessant and deprecating brain chatter – which you may recognise. While you can allow your mind to wander, eventually you will be forced to observe and interact with your environment. Whether you are weeding, pruning, or pricking out seedlings, you become absorbed in your work and have to pay attention. This allows you to become more rooted, more open to finding joy and ultimately, much more resilient to life's ups and downs.

Nature, it seems is therefore not only the best gardener, but she also is happy enough to work as a team player, as long as we are firmly on her side, that we try not to usurp her authority and are willing to learn from her deep well of knowledge. The key to successful gardening is less about how much you can do and a lot about how much you can pay attention. This is the key to learning. Furthermore, I have discovered that her talents go beyond gardening, as she is also an amazing life coach. She frequently raises her eyebrows at me when I am wrestling with a problem in my life and asks me to consider things from her perspective. 'Look at this,' she urges, showing me her treasures, and after a while I slowly begin to understand what she means. Finally, I am most grateful for nature's role as a healer, a mender of broken hearts, shattered dreams and failing bodies. Without her, I would most likely be fulfilling my doctors' expectations of being homebound, unable to work and relying on daytime TV for distraction. Instead, I have been able to create, at least in part, the life I had once dreamed of. It's not perfect by any means and sometimes, like many things in life, it brings me sadness and pain. Yet despite all this, gardening for me has been an anchor, a respite, a metaphor for life, an adventure and an income. For those reasons alone, I am forever in her debt.

With every simple act of gardening and planting, we affirm our stake in the future. It's a declaration of optimism, hope and love. I was talking to a woman once, while out walking in the woods, who told me that she believed that gardening would save the world. I hope she's right. I really do. That would be like alchemy.